Anonymous

Digest of Laws Relating to Free Schools in the State of Arkansas

Anonymous

Digest of Laws Relating to Free Schools in the State of Arkansas

ISBN/EAN: 9783744693233

Printed in Europe, USA, Canada, Australia, Japan

Cover: Foto ©ninafisch / pixelio.de

More available books at **www.hansebooks.com**

DIGEST OF LAWS

RELATING TO

FREE SCHOOLS

IN THE

STATE OF ARKANSAS,

AND

FORMS FOR USE OF SCHOOL OFFICERS,

COMPILED AND ANNOTATED BY JUNIUS JORDAN, SUPER-
INTENDENT OF PUBLIC INSTRUCTION.

BY AUTHORITY.

LITTLE ROCK, ARK.:
THE BROWN PRINTING COMPANY.
1895

CHAPTER CXXXIX

OF

SANDELS & HILL'S DIGEST.

SECTION

FREE SCHOOLS—SUPPORT OF.

6930. The state ever to maintain free schools; who may receive gratuitous instruction.

6931. State taxes for support of; limit; *per capita* tax; additional taxation may be in school districts; limit.

COMMON SCHOOL FUND.

6932. What moneys and other property constitute this fund; to be invested.
6933. County courts may place certain funds to credit of school districts, when.
6634. Principal arising from sale of sixteenth sections shall not be apportioned or used.
6935. Certain townships, when not entitled to proceeds.
6936. Income of fund and *per capita* tax, how appropriated.
6937. Auditor to draw warrant on treasurer for school revenues due the counties, when.
6938. County collector to collect *per capita* tax and pay into county treasury, when and how.
6939. Debts due the fund by estates preferred.
6940. No costs to be charged in suits for dues to the fund, when.

COMMISSIONERS OF SCHOOL FUND.

6941. Board of commissioners, who compose; when and where to meet.
6942. Governor to be president of board.
6943. Superintendent of public instruction to be secretary and keep record of proceedings; copy of record to be evidence.
6944. Board to invest fund in bonds.
6945. Suits for moneys due the fund may be in any court having jurisdiction, when; board may direct officer to prosecute suit.
6946. All moneys accruing to the fund to be paid into treasury; how paid out.
6947. Auditor accountant for board; to make report, when and to whom.

6948. Auditor to draw warrants on the fund to pay for investments, when.
6949. Treasurer to pay such warrants and keep in treasury all securities so purchased.
6950. Board to make settlements with the state treasurer, when.

SUPERVISION OF PUBLIC SCHOOLS.

6951. General assembly to provide officers for.

STATE SUPERINTENDENT OF PUBLIC INSTRUCTION.

6952. When elected
6953. Oath of.
6954. To have general superintendency of the schools of the state.
6955. Office to be at Little Rock; have all books, etc., of his department there, and of all the business of his office keep a record.
6956, 6957, 6958, 6959, 6960, 6961, 6962, 6963. Duties and powers of.
6964. Report to governor, when.
6965. Governor to transmit report to general assembly.
6966. Superintendent to have his reports published and distributed.
6967, 6968, 6969, 6970, 6971. Powers and duties; further specifications of.
6972. Vacancy in office of superintendent, how filled.
6973. Superintendent or examiner acting as book agent, or receiving pay for influence, guilty of misdemeanor.
6974. Superintendent may grant state certificates to any person passing an examination.
6975. May prepare list of text-books and recommend same.
6976. Impression of superintendent's seal of office to be furnished to secretary of state.
6977. Documents, etc., in superintendent's office, how to be authenticated.
6978. To prepare forms for grades of certificates to teachers, school registers, reports of directors and examiners.

DISTRICT NORMAL SCHOOLS.

6979, 6980, 6981, 6982, 6983. Changed to county normals by act of April 20, 1895.

SCHOOL DISTRICTS.

6984. Repealed.
6985. When change proposed, notice to be given; how, where and when posted.
6986. Schools to be body corporate; name of; corporate powers.
6987. To have property in corporate name.
6988. No district to be formed, nor old one reduced, so as to contain less than thirty persons of scholastic age.
6989. County court may form new districts or change boundaries; when.
6990. Such territory to have requisite children or property.
6991. Proportional share of debt to be adjusted.
6992. Proportionate share of surplus fund to be adjusted.

SCHOOL LAWS.

APPORTIONMENT OF SCHOOL FUND.

6993. County court to apportion school revenue to the districts; rule.
6994. New districts, when and how to be apportioned.
6995. County examiners to report number of residents in each district.
6996. County clerks to lay reports before the court.
6997. Counties losing funds by change of boundaries, to be reimbursed.
6998. Amounts thus paid deducted from share of what counties.
6999. Auditor to draw warrant for county's share of school fund, when.

COUNTY EXAMINERS.

7000. How appointed, commissioned, etc.
7001. Appointments heretofore made validated.
7002. Oath of.
7003. To stand examination before entering on duties.
7004. No one to fill the office of examiner and school director at the same time.
7005. Clerk to notify superintendent of appointment, etc.
7006. Superintendent to examine, or appoint some one to examine him; questions to be used.
7007. Salary of; limit to.
7008. Examiner not to examine applicant till fee is paid to treasurer, etc.
7009. Duty of examiner.
7010. Examination, what to consist of.
7011. Examiner to give certificates according to grade to those entitled.
7012. Shall not license certain persons described.
7013. May cite for re-examination and revoke licenses; when.
7014. Effect of such revocation.
7015. Additional examination in regard to land surveys.
7016. Failure to teach the instructions required in preceding section, cause to revoke licenses.
7017. To issue three grades of certificates.
7018. To keep record of teachers licensed.
7019. To encourage inhabitants to establish public schools; report to state superintendent condition of schools in his county, etc.
7020. Annual report of, what to contain.
7021. To number the school districts and keep record and description of each.
7022. May appoint person to hold institutes and examinations, when.
7023. County judge may remove examiner and appoint successor, when.
7024. Examiner failing to perform required duties; forfeiture.
7025. Examiner to present, and may have allowed, by the county court, an account; of what; how much allowed.
7026. How paid.

ANNUAL SCHOOL MEETING.

7027, 7028. When held; who may vote.
7029. Quorum; routine of business.

7030. Annual district election, how held; judges and clerks of.
7031. Ballot, form of; returns, how made.
7032. Result of election to be delivered to county clerk.
7033. County court to open returns and determine amount of taxes voted.
7034. Taxes so voted, how levied and collected.

SCHOOL DIRECTORS.

7035. When elected; term of office.
7036. Judges to give certificate within five days; director to qualify within ten days thereafter; filing certificate and oath.
7037. Oath of office, by whom administered.
7038, 7039. Refusal to qualify as director, forfeiture; failing to perform duties of his office, forfeiture.
7040. Vacancy in office of director, how filled.
7041, 7042, 7043. Directors, board of; duties and powers.
7044. Month, meaning of, in school law.
7045. Directors may expend annually not more than twenty-five dollars for charts, etc.
7046, 7047, 7048, 7049, 7050, 7051. Directors, board of; further specification of duties and powers.
7052. Warrant drawn by directors; county treasurer to pay.
7053. Directors to give notice of annual school meeting; contents of notice.
7054, 7055. Director, one to be clerk at all district meetings, and keep record of proceedings; also to keep the yearly accounts of the district.
7056. Directors to report to county clerk the officers elected and amount of money voted at annual meeting.
7057. Directors to report annually to county examiner; contents of report.
7058. Directors failing to make this report, liable in damages.
7059. Directors to settle annually with county treasurer.
7060, 7061. Directors may suspend any pupil for cause; may permit older persons to attend school.
7062, 7063, 7064. County court may transfer scholars to an adjoining district, when; regulations concerning such transfer.
7065. Directors may permit private school to be taught in district school house, when.
7066. Directors may cause schools to be closed. when.
7067. Directors and examiners exempt from road work.
7068. Neglect to report tax levied at annual meeting liability for loss; fine.
7069. Directors to furnish county clerk with list of all persons owning property in the district liable to pay special tax, when.
7070. Neglect of any duty under school laws, fine for.

TEACHERS.

7071. Must have certificate and license to teach, or not entitled to pay.
7072. Must keep daily register.

SCHOOL LAWS.

7073. Duty of, to attend teachers' institute.
7074. Not to permit sectarian books to be used in school.
7075. How paid; preference of claim
7076. To return register, else pay stopped.

TRESPASS ON SCHOOL HOUSE, ETC.

7077. Injuring school house, fixtures, etc., fine for.

SCHOOL WARRANTS—DISBURSEMENT OF FUNDS, ETC.

7078. County collectors and treasurers not to be interested in school warrants.
7079. District school tax payable in warrants of district.
7080. County treasurer to keep register of school warrants, how.
7081. County treasurer to give notice of receipt of school funds; how such funds paid out.
7082. Officer failing to comply with act, punishment.
7083. Director fraudulently issuing warrant, punishment.
7084. County treasurer to report school funds received by him, disbursements and balance in treasury, when.
7085. Orders of directors to be presented to treasurer, when; order of payment.
7086. If not paid, how indorsed; record of such warrants.

VIOLATION OF SCHOOL LAWS—DUTY OF PROSECUTING ATTORNEYS.

7087. Prosecuting attorneys, when school laws are violated, to bring offenders to trial; compensation; costs in such cases.

SPECIAL ACTS FOR SCHOOLS IN CITIES AND TOWNS.

7088. Cities and towns may be special districts.
7089, 7090. Procedure to adopt the act and elect directors.
7091. Election in, when and how held.
7092. By whom held, duties, compensation and oath of judges and clerks.
7093. Polls, when opened and closed.
7094. If a regular judge fails to appear, when and how judge elected.
7095. When electors vote.
7096. Returns of election.
7097. Duty of clerk; duty of county clerk.
7098. Directors, when and how to qualify.
7099. Provisions of chapter not applicable.
7100. Board to organize, how.
7101. Meetings of board; quorum; board may make rules for its own government.
7102, 7103. Powers and duties of board.
7104. Warrants on the county treasury, how drawn and signed.
7105. Secretary of board, duties of, compensation.
7106. Title to all school property vested in city or town as a school district, and to be under control of directors.
7107. Name of district; corporate powers; style of board.

7108. Debts of former districts to be paid.
7109. Directors failing to qualify or to perform their official duties; penalty.
7110. Board of visitors and examiners, how appointed; term of office; appointee failing to perform duties; penalty.
7111. District to receive full share of school fund.
7112. State superintendent to make suggestions, etc., to directors.
7113. Provisions of the general school law; when to apply to special districts; county court may annex contiguous territory, when.

II. SCHOOL LANDS.

SECTION
7114. Inhabitants of any congressional township may petition for sale of sixteenth section.
7115. Duties of collector on receipt of petition.
7116. If subdividing no tract shall contain more than forty acres.
7117. Collector shall cause each subdivision to be appraised.
7118. Collector shall give public notice of time of sale.
7119. Collector shall offer each tract separately. Sale shall take place between the hours of 12 m. and 3 p. m., and may be continued from day to day. No tract shall be sold for less than appraisement. If any tract remain unsold collector may without petition sell again, giving notice of sale.
7120. Collector shall report sales to county court.—If sales not confirmed court shall direct collector to advertise and sell again. Form of certificate to be given to purchaser. Commissioner of state lands shall make deed on presentation of certificate.
7121. Collector shall pay all costs of sales out of proceeds.
7122. County clerk shall ascertain who are paying taxes on the sixteenth sections; other duties.
7123. County clerk shall keep the account of each township entitled to benefits from this act.
7124. Penalty imposed on county clerk for failing to keep record.
7125. Collection of claims due common school fund; authorizes attorney general to employ competent attorneys in each county to collect claims due on account of sixteenth section; other duties.
7126. State treasurer shall place to credit of proper county all moneys received on account of sixteenth section lands.
7127. State treasurer to invest money and place accrued interest to credit of each county.
7128. Accrued interest may be drawn in same manner as now provided for by law.
7129. All evidences of indebtedness arising from sales of sixteenth sections shall be turned over to commissioner of state lands.
7130. County collectors and treasurers shall turn over to state treasurer all the moneys in their hands belonging to 15th section fund.

7131. Commissioner of state lands shall keep record of all deeds made for sixteenth section lands.

PATENTS.

7132. Last assignee of certificate for school lands entitled to deed, when
7133. Auditor to execute deed for school lands to heirs at law, when.
7134. Lands so conveyed, to stand charged with amount advanced by estate to procure title.
7135. Patents issued, and all official acts done during the war concerning school lands, made valid.
7136. Rights of the state in such lands, acquired under judgment, etc., where deeds had been made to purchasers, vested in the proper owners under such deeds.
7137. Certain suits by the state for school lands to be dismissed.
7138. Commissioner of state lands to make deed for school lands paid for, and for which no conveyance has been made.

LEASE OF SCHOOL LANDS.

7139. Collector to lease school lands, when.
7140. Manner and terms of leasing.
7141. Notice of leasing, how given.
7142. Leased by private contract, when.
7143. Occupants to pay rent.
7144. Lessees, rules governing, minimum rent.

I. SCHOOLS.

FREE SCHOOLS—SUPPORT OF.

SECTION 6930. Intelligence and virtue being the safeguards of liberty, and the bulwark of a free and good government, the state shall ever maintain a general, suitable and efficient system of free schools, whereby all persons in the state, between the ages of six and twenty-one years, may receive gratuitous instruction.

SEC. 6931. The general assembly shall provide, by general laws, for the support of common schools by taxes, which shall never exceed in any one year two mills on the dollar on the taxable property of the state ; and by an annual *per capita* tax of one dollar, to be assessed on every male inhabitant of this state over the age of twenty-one years. *Provided*, The general assembly may, by general law, authorize school districts to levy, by a vote of the qualified electors of such districts, a tax not to exceed five mills on the dollar in any one year for school purposes. *Provided, further,* That no such tax shall be appropriated to any other purpose, nor to any other district, than that for which it was levied. *Art. 14, secs. 1 and 3, Const.*

POWER TO TAX FOR SCHOOL PURPOSES.

The state is the source of authority. "Every muncipal corporation and every political division of the state must be able to show due authority from the state to make the demand."

Cooley on Taxation, 474.

School districts are civil corporations, and the legislature may confer upon them the power to tax for school purposes.

State v. Bremond, 38 *Texas,* 116.

The words "public schools" are synonymous with "common schools," and mean the schools created by law and maintained at the public expense, and which are open and common to the children of the inhabitants alike.

Jenkins v. Andover, 103 *Mass.,* 94.
People v. Board of Education, 13 *Barb.* (*N. Y.*), 490.
Holbert v. Sparks, 9 *Bush,* 259.
Webster's Dictionary, Common Schools.
Henderson v. Collins and Jett, Kentucky Reports.
Abbott's Law Dictionary, title, Common Schools.

Taxation for public schools is for a public use and purpose, and public education is a fit and appropriate object of taxation.

68 *M. E.,* 582.
Williams v. School District, 33 *Vt.,* 271.
Marshall v. Donovan, 10 *Buch.* (*Ky.*), 681.
6 *Cowen* (*N. Y.*), 543.
56 *Pa. St.* 359; 22 *Grattan* (*Va.*), 857.

There can be no taxation in aid of a private educational institution operated for individual profit.

Curtis' Admr's v. Whipple, 24 *Wis.,* 350.
Philadelphia Assn. v. Wood, 39 *Pa. St.,* 73.

That a school building was larger than was immediately needed, and that the vote specified among other uses of a part of the building, that of holding school society meetings and lectures therein, does not vitaite the tax, nor authorize a court to enjoin the same.

Sheldon v. Centre School District, 25 *Conn.,* 224.
Greenbanks v. Boutwell, 43 *Vt.,* 207.

In New Hampshire it has been held that a vote by a school district to remove

SCHOOL LAWS.

and repair a school house came within the authority granted by statute to raise money " for erecting and repairing school houses."

Bump v. State, 4 (*N. H.*), 48.

Taxation to support high schools and normal schools has been declared proper and lawful unless absolutely restricted by the constitution.

Stuart v. School District, 30 *Mich.*, 69.
Report U. S. Com'r Ed. for 1876-7.
Richards v. Raymond, Supt. Court of Illinois, Nov. 10, 1879.
Chicago Legal News, Vol. 12, *No.* 11.
Merrick and others v. Inhabitants of Newburyport, 10 *Metcalf* (*Mass.*), 508.
Briggs et al. v. Johnson County, Mo., 4 *Dillon C. C. R.*, 148.
Commonwealth v. Dedham, 16 *Mass.*, 141.
Commonwealth v. Sheffield, 11 *Cush* (*Mass.*), 178.
Jenkins v. Andover, 103 *Mass.*, 94.

In a Massachusetts case it was decided that money raised for the support of a female high school for the purpose of teaching book-keeping, algebra, geometry, history, rhetoric, mental, moral and natural philosophy, botany, the Latin and French languages, was lawfully raised by taxation.

10 *Metcalf* (*Mass.*), 508.

Because a constitution expressly names free schools and a university, and does not name normal schools, is no constitutional reason against taxation to establish normal schools.

Briggs v. Johnson County, 4 *Dill., C. C. R.*, 148.

COMMON SCHOOL FUND.

SEC. 6932. The proceeds of all lands that have been, or hereafter may be, granted by the United States to this state, and not otherwise appropriated by the United States or this state; also all moneys, stocks, bonds, lands and other property now belonging to any fund for purposes of education; also the net proceeds of all sales of lands and other property and effects that may accrue to this state by escheat, or from sales of estrays, or from unclaimed dividends, or distributive shares of the estates of deceased persons; also any proceeds of the sale of public lands which may have been, or may be hereafter, paid over to the state (congress consenting); also ten per cent of the net proceeds of the sales of all state lands; also all the grants, gifts or devises that have been or hereafter may be made to this state, and not otherwise appropriated by the tenure of the grant, gift or devise, shall be securely invested and sacredly preserved as a public school fund that shall be designated as the " common school fund " of the state, and which shall be the common property of the state, except the proceeds arising from the sale or lease of the sixteenteen section (*a*). *Act December 7, 1875, sec. 1.*

SEC. 6933. The county courts of the various counties are authorized and empowered to place to the credit of the common school fund of the county, any and all school funds that may be in the county treasury, derived from various sources, and about which there is any doubt as to their proper application with the county court, and that said school funds, when so placed to the credit of the common school fund, shall be, by said county courts, apportioned among the school districts of the county as is now provided by law.

SEC. 6934. The principal arising from the sale of the sixteenth section of land shall never be apportioned or used.

SEC. 6935. Should any of the funds mentioned in this act arise from the sale of said sixteenth section of land and there should be any doubt as to the township from whence it came, then such townships as have not disposed of the sixteenth section of land, or may have disposed of the same and have the proceeds placed to their credit, shall not be entitled to any part of the interest arising from said doubtful sixteenth section fund. *Act March 13, 1885, secs. 1, 2.*

SEC. 6936. The annual income from the said fund, together with one dollar *per capita* to be annually assessed on every male inhabitant over the age of twenty-one years, and so much of the ordinary annual revenues of the state as may hereafter be set apart by law for such purposes, shall be

---

(*a*) No money or property belonging to the public school fund, or to this state, for the benefit of schools or universities, shall ever be used for any other than for the respective purposes to which it belongs. *Art.* 14, *sec.* 2, *Const.*

faithfully appropriated for maintaining a system of free common schools for this state, and shall be appropriated to no other purpose whatever. *Act December 7, 1875, sec. 2.*

SEC. 6937. The state auditor shall, on requisition from the state superintendent of public instruction, draw warrants on the state treasurer for payment to the several county treasurers of the school revenues due their respective counties.

SEC. 6938. The *per capita* tax levied by the general revenue laws of the state shall be collected by the county collector at the same time and place that the state taxes are collected, and be paid in the county treasury on or before the first day of July of each year, in the presence of the county conrt clerk, who shall make a record of the same as a revenue for the support of common schools (*b*). *Ib., secs. 31 and 32.*

SEC. 6939. In the payment of debts by executors and administrators, the debts due the common school fund shall have a preference over all other debts, except funeral and other expenses attending the last sickness.

SEC. 6940. No justice of the peace, constable, clerk of a court or sheriff shall charge any costs in any suit where the collector or any other officer sues for the recovery of any money due to the common school fund, if the plaintiff in such cause is unsuccessful. *Act January 11, 1853, secs. 50 and 55.*

COMMISSIONERS OF SCHOOL FUND.

SEC. 6941. The secretary of state, auditor and state superintendent of public instruction shall constitute a board of commissioners of the common school fund, and shall meet semi-annually at the office of said superintendent on the first Monday in February and on the first Monday in August in each year. *Provided,* The secretary of state may

---

(*b.*) The penalty collected for the non-payment of taxes on personal property is to be paid into the county school fund. See *sec.* 6589.

assemble the members of said board any time at his discretion.

Sec. 6942. The secretary of state shall be president of said board and shall sign the journal of each day's proceedings. *Act Dec. 7, 1875, secs. 3, 4, as amended by act April 10, 1893.*

Sec. 6943. The superintendent of public instruction shall act as secretary of the said board, and shall keep a faithful, correct record of the proceedings, and shall keep the said record open at all times for inspection. A copy of said record, certified by the secretary of the board, shall be in all cases received as evidence equal with the original.

Sec. 6944. The said board of school commissioners shall have the management and investment of the common school fund belonging to the state, and shall from time to time, as the same may accumulate, securely invest the said funds in bonds of the United States or the state of Arkansas.

Sec. 6945. That all moneys required by law to be paid into the treasury to the credit of the common school fund may, if the same be not paid within thirty days after they shall have become due and payable, be recovered, with interest due thereon, by action in any court having jurisdiction; and such action shall be prosecuted by the attorney general of the state, or by the prosecuting attorney of any judicial district within this state, when directed by the said board.*

Sec. 6946. All moneys belonging or owing to the common school fund, as mentioned in section 6932, or accruing as revenues therefrom, together with the state school tax, shall be paid directly into the state treasury, and shall not be paid out except on the warrant of the auditor. *Act December 7, 1875, secs. 5-8.*

Sec. 6947. The state auditor shall be the accountant of said board, and shall, annually, on the first Monday in Oc-

---

*See *Orr v. State*, 56-107.

SCHOOL LAWS. 15

tober, transmit to the governor and to the superintendent of public instruction a report of the condition of the school fund on the 1st day of July last preceding, with an abstract of the accounts thereof in his office.

SEC. 6948. The auditor shall, under the direction of the board of commissioners, draw warrants on the state treasurer for the payment of all or any portion of the common school fund belonging to the state, for the purchase of bonds or other securities in which the same is by law invested.

SEC. 6949. The state treasurer shall, by virtue of such warrant, pay from the uninvested common school fund the purchase money for said securities, and shall receive and deposit the same in the state treasury for safe-keeping, and receipt to the president of the board of commissioners for the kind and amount of such securities.

SEC. 6950. The said board shall, at their semi-annual meeting, settle with the state treasurer all accounts of the common school fund not before settled. *Ib., secs. 9-12.*

SUPERVISION OF PUBLIC SCHOOLS.

SEC. 6951. The supervision of public schools, and the execution of the laws regulating the same, shall be vested in and confided to such officers as may be provided for by the general assembly. *Art. 14, sec. 4, Const.*

STATE SUPERINTENDENT OF PUBLIC INSTRUCTION.

SEC. 6952. At the next general election, and every two years thereafter, there shall be elected a state superintendent of public instruction, by the qualified electors of this state, as state officers are now elected.

SEC. 6953. Before entering upon the duties of his office, he shall take and subscribe the oath prescribed for officers by the constitution of this state, and shall file such oath with the secretary of state.

SEC. 6954. The superintendent of public instruction shall

be charged with the general superintendence of the business relating to the free common schools of this state.*

SEC. 6955. He shall open at the seat of the state government (at the expense of the state) a suitable office, in which he shall keep all books, reports, documents and other papers pertaining to his department, and where he shall be in attendance when not necessarily absent on business, and have personal supervision of the business affairs of his office, and keep a clear and correct record thereof.

SEC. 6956. He shall furnish suitable questions† for the examination of teachers to the county examiner; he shall hold a teachers' institute annually in each judicial district of the state, to be called a normal district institute; he shall arrange the programme exercises for each of such institutes, and preside thereat. *Provided*, If he should not be present, the teachers who may have assembled may organize and hold such normal district institute. (See recent act of the legislature placed in the digest after sec. 6978.)

SEC. 6957. He shall prepare and transmit to the county examiners, school registers, blank certificates, reports and other printed blanks, together with other suitable blanks, forms and printed instructions, to be forwarded to directors and other school officers, as may be necessary to aid such officers in making their reports and carrying into full effect

---

*A general power of charge and supervision oi schools includes the power to make all reasonable rules and regulations for the discipline, government and arrangements of schools. 5 *Cush.* (*Mass.*), 198 ; 8 *Cush.* (*Mass.*), 160; 12 *All.* (*Mass.*), 127; 105 *Mass.*, 476; 63 *Ill.*, 353; 71 *Mo.*, 628; 13 *Brad.*, 520.

As to what is a reasonable rule, see 63 *Ill.*, 353; 48 *Vt.*, 476, 477; 31 *Iowa*, 565. It is in short, "Any rule of the school or system not subversive of the rights of the children or parents or in conflict with humanity and the precepts of divine law which leads to advance the law in establishing public schools."

†The state superintendent is the only one authorized to furnish questions for these examinations. The examinations held by examiners at the close of a private school of their own, in which they have prepared the teachers to answer certain questions prepared by the examiner for the occasion, are not legal, and a license granted in this manner is void.

the various provisions of the school laws of this state. *Act December 7, 1875, secs. 13-16.*

SEC. 6958. The superintendent of public instruction shall prepare a form of poll books to be used by the directors of the various school districts of this state at their annual elections as are now, or may hereafter be provided by law, and have the same printed as other blanks for school purposes; and shall transmit the same to the county examiner of each county for distribution to school directors in the same manner as other school blanks are now, or shall hereafter be distributed. *Act March 2, 1887.*

SEC. 6959. He shall exercise such supervision over the school funds as to ascertain the amount and disposal made of the same, their protection and safety when invested or deposited, and recommend measures for their seecurity and preservation, and for rendering them most productive of revenues; shall enforce the strict application of the school revenues to the legitimate purposes for which they were intended, and shall, when directed by the commissioners of the school fund, cause to be instituted, in the name of the state of Arkansas, suits or actions for the recovery of any portion of the said funds or said revenues that may be squandered, illegally applied or unsafely deposited.

SEC. 6960. He shall, on or before the first day of November in each year, prepare and submit to the governor of this state an annual report, in writing, showing the number of persons between the ages of six and twenty-one years residing in the state on the first day of the preceding July; the number of such persons in each county; the number of each sex; the number of white; the number of colored; the whole number of such persons that attended the free common schools of the state during the year ending the thirtieth day of the last preceding June, and the number in each county that attended during the same period; the number of whites of each sex that attended, and the number of colored of each sex that attended the said schools; the number of common schools in the state ; the number of pupils that studied each of the branches taught ; the average wages paid teachers of each sex ; the relative average wages paid to male and female teachers respectively, according to the different grades of their certificates ; the number of school houses erected during the year ; the material and cost thereof; the number previously erected, the material of which they were constructed, their condition and value ; the number with their grounds inclosed ; the counties in which teachers' institutes were held, and the number that attended the institutes in each county.

SEC. 6961. He shall likewise report the amount of permanent school fund belonging to the state at the close of the fiscal school year, and the amount of other property apportioned to school purposes ; the nature, kind and amount of such investments made of the same ; the safety and permanency of such investments ; the amount of revenue accruing from the school funds ; the income received from the *per capita* assessments of each county, and the amount derived from such assessment in all the counties of the state ; the income derived from all other sources, together with the amount derived from each ; likewise in what sums, for what purposes and in what manner the said school revenue shall have been expended, and what amount of school moneys of various kinds are in the various county treasuries unexpended.

SEC. 6962. He shall include in his report such plans as he may have matured for the improvement of the common school system of this state ; for the accumulation, the investment and the more judicious management of the common school fund, and, when he may deem it advisable, shall recommend measures for a more economical and advantageous collection and expenditure of the revenues accruing from the said fund ; and whenever it comes to his knowledge that any of the investments of the school funds are not safe, or that any portion of the said fund is liable to be lost, that it is unproductive of revenue, or that any of the school revenues have been diverted from their proper channel or from the appropriate objects contemplated, he shall report the facts to the governor and to the general assembly, if in session.

SEC. 6963. He shall also append to his report a statistical table, compiled from the materials transmitted to his office by school officers, with proper summaries, averages and totals given.

SEC. 6964. He shall present such a comparison of results, and such an exhibit of his administration, and of the operation of the common free school system, together with such statements of the true condition of the schools of the state, as shall distinctly show the improvements and progress made from year to year in the department of public instruction.

SEC. 6965. The annual reports of the state superintendent to the governor shall be transmitted by the governornor to the general assembly at the opening of the session.

SEC. 6966. He shall have his reports to the governor published as soon as practicable after they have been made, and shall cause them to be distributed among the various school officers of the state, to be kept on file in their respective offices. *Provided*, He shall not have more than five thousand copies of such reports printed for any one year, the printing of such reports to be let out as other contracts for printing. *Act December 7, 1875, secs. 16–23.*

SEC. 6967. He shall on the first Monday of August and on the first Monday of February of each year, make a *pro rata* apportionment to the several counties of the state of the remaining revenues in the state treasury available for distribution for school purposes, on the basis of the number of persons between the ages of six and twenty-one years, residing in said county, respectively, on the first day of September previous; and he shall publish a statement of the same, and as early as practicable, shall transmit a copy thereof to each county examiner and to each of the several treasurers in the state, and to each county clerk, who shall submit the same to the county court at its next term; and he shall thereupon draw his requisition on the state auditor in favor of the treasurers of the several counties for such amount as the said counties may be entitled to receive for the support of free common schools. *Act March 20, 1891.*

SEC. 6968. He shall, from time to time, publish in convenient pamphlet form, and furnish each school officer, the acts of the general assembly relating to common schools, and the decisions of the courts having competent jurisdiction in relation to the school laws ; and he shall likewise, at the request of any school officer, render a decision relating to the intent, construction or administration of any portion of the school laws on which decisions shall not have been published, and he may, when he shall deem it advisable to have the opinion of the attorney general, require said opinion to be given in writing(*a*).

SEC. 6969. He shall, for the purpose of ascertaining the amounts, safety and preservation of the school funds, have access to the auditor's books and papers, with full power to use and inspect the same.

SEC. 6970. At the expiration of his term of office he shall deliver to his successor possession of his office, together with all books, records, documents, papers and other articles belonging or pertaining to his office.

SEC. 6971. He shall affix the seal of the department of

(*a*.) It is the sole duty of the superintendent of public instruction to render decisions relating to the intent, construction or administration of any portion of the school laws. The attorney general is the legal adviser of the superintendent. and not of school officers.

·public instruction to all official communications from his office.

SEC. 6972. Whenever a vacancy in the office of superintendent of public instruction shall occur, from death, resignation or otherwise, the governor shall appoint a person of suitable attainments to serve the remainder of the unexpired term. *Provided,* Such vacancy shall occur within nine months from the next succeeding election; otherwise, an election shall be ordered, as in case of state officers.

SEC. 6973. Neither the state superintendent nor county examiner shall act as agent for any author, publisher or bookseller, nor directly or indirectly receive any gift, emolument, reward or promise of reward for his influence in recommending or procuring the use of any book, school apparatus or furniture of any kind whatever, in any public school; and any school officer who shall violate the provisions of this section shall be deemed guilty of a misdemeanor, and subject to removal from office. *Act December 7, 1875, secs. 25-30.*

SEC. 6974. The state superintendent of public instruction shall have power to grant state certificates, which shall be valid for life, unless revoked, to any person in the state who shall pass a thorough examination in all those branches required for granting county certificates; and, also, in algebra and geometry, physics, rhetoric, mental philosophy, history, Latin, the constitutions of the United States and of the state of Arkansas, natural history and theory and art of teaching.

State license can not be granted without an examination. No provision is made whereby a college diploma or the diploma of a normal school becomes the equivalent for a state license. There is no legal method whereby a state license may be secured save by an examination. These examinations are public and conducted at the office of the state superintendent.

The law does not fix a minimum age nor require experience. But it was never the intent of the legislature to put immature and inexperienced boys and girls in charge of schools, much less give them a life license. In all other departments of the law, minors are called infants, and made subject to disabilities and to the control of parents and guardians. Maturity of mind and srtength of character are requisites for the successful determination and management of the important questions arising in school life. Applicants for state license must be of legal age and have a successful experience of at least twenty months in the school room. The oral and written methods are combined in the examination.

The oral is adapted to disclose—
1. Skill in expedients.
2. Aptness in illustration.
3. Manner of expression, etc.

The written is expected to show—
1. Habits of thinking.
2. Modes of reasoning.
3. Discipline of the mind.
4. Accuracy.
5. Acquaintance with principles.
6. Availability of knowledge.
7. Knowledge itself.

SEC. 6975. He shall prepare, for the benefit of the common schools of the state, a list of such text-books on orthography, reading in English, mental and written arithmetic, penmanship, English grammar, modern geography and history of the United States as are best adapted to the wants of the learner, and as have been prepared with reference to the most philosophical methods of teaching those branches, and shall recommend the said text-books to teachers and to directors throughout the state.

The following are deduced from an opinion of the attorney general:
1. That the list is to be determined by the state superintendent.
2. That the directors in adopting books are limited to the list.
3. That books not upon the list cannot be required in any school of the state supported by public funds.

SEC. 6976. He shall procure and adopt a seal for his office, and furnish an impression and description of said seal to the secretary of state, to be preserved in his office.

SEC. 6977. A copy of any paper or document deposited or filed in the office of the superintendent of public instruction shall, when authenticated by the said seal, be evidence equal, to all intents and purposes, with the original.

SCHOOL LAWS. 23

SEC. 6978. The said superintendent shall prepare appropriate forms for three several grades of certificates to be issued to teachers by the county examiners. He shall prepare suitable school registers, in which teachers, at the close of the school term, are to make their reports to the trustees of the name and age of each pupil, the date of each pupil's entrance, the separate days on which each attended school, the studies each pursued, the total attendance; and shall likewise prepare suitable forms for the reports of directors and county examiners. *Act December 7, 1875, secs. 33-37.*

This register must be kept by each public school teacher according to the forms prescribed, before any charge can be made for services.

By a subsequent act the superintendent is required to furnish poll-books for the school districts.

COUNTY NORMAL INSTITUTES.

Be it enacted by the General Assembly of the State of Arkansas:

SECTION 1. That the state superintendent of public instruction is hereby authorized and empowered to arrange for the establishment of county normal institutes for the white teachers of Arkansas, or for such white persons as desire to become teachers in the public schools of this state, being one for each county of the state, and such additional ones for the colored teachers at such places as may be selected by the superintendent.

SEC. 2. That said superintendent shall select a principal for each normal institute, arrange a programme for its daily work, and formulate such rules and regulations therefor as shall best conduce to the interests of the institute and to the faithful execution of this law. The course of study shall comprise a thorough drill upon the principles of the common school branches, history and constitution of Arkansas, and such pedagogical instruction as shall fully develop the teachers' professional, general, moral and social preparation for work in the public schools; special attention shall be given to organization, arrangement of pupils, use of text-books, classification, programmes, use of school devices and apparatus, discipline, punishment and the purposes of punishment, also upon the different methods of presenting the different subjects to be taught in the schools, having more direct reference to the rural than to the town schools.

SEC. 3. Each of said schools shall last for a consecutive term of twenty days each, of each year, at such time and place as may be agreed upon by the state superintendent and county examiner. Other pupils of suitable age and advancement may be admitted to these institutes at the discretion of the state superintendent and county examiner.

SEC. 4. For the purpose of carrying this law into effect, the sum of ten thousand dollars per annum for the next two years, is hereby appropriated out of any moneys in the treasury not otherwise appropriated; *Provided*, That an itemized bill shall be presented by each instructor employed in these institutes, together with a certificate from the superintendent of public instruction, to the auditor of state, who shall thereupon draw his warrant for the same; *Provided, further*, That no part of this appropriation shall be used for any purpose other than the payment of instructors.

SEC. 5. This law shall take effect from and after its passage.

Approved April 20, 1895.

Though this law does not repeal the district normal law, there is no provision made for carrying it into effect, and it is now a useless statute.

SCHOOL DISTRICTS.

Be it enacted by the General Assembly of the State of Arkansas:

SECTION 1. The county courts of this state shall have power to dissolve any school district now established, or which may hereafter be established in its county and attach the territory thereof in whole or in part to an adjoining district or districts, whenever a majority of the electors residing in such district shall petition the court so to do.

SEC. 2. When such dissolution is proposed, notice shall

be given by those proposing the same by posters in four public places in the district. Said notices to be posted thirty days before the meeting of the term of the court at which such petition is proposed to be presented.

SEC. 3. Whenever, under this act, any district shall be abolished, any indebtedness due by it, or funds on hand to its credit shall be proportioned by the court among the districts to which its territory has been attached, according to the value of the territory each received, of which action of dissolution and distribution of indebtedness or funds, as the case may be, the clerk of the court shall give due notice to directors of each district affected, showing the territory attached to their district, and amount of indebtedness adjudged against it, or funds credited to it, as the case may be.

SEC. 4. The directors of the district dissolved, upon receipt of notice of clerk, shall transmit, without delay, all of the records of said district to the county examiner of the county for preservation in his office.

SEC. 5. That section 6984 of Sandels & Hill's Digest be and the same is hereby repealed.

SEC. 6. All laws in conflict herewith are hereby repealed, and this act take effect and be in force from and after its passage.

Approved April 1, 1895.

SEC. 6985. When a change is proposed in any school district notice shall be given by the parties proposing the change, by putting up hand bills in four or more conspicuous places in each district to be affected, one of said notices to be placed on the public school building in each affected district. All of said notices to be posted thirty days before the convening of the court to which they propose to present their petition ; said notices shall give a geographical description of the proposed change. *Act April 8, 1891.*

SEC. 6986. Each school district shall be a body corporate, by the name and style of "School District No.———, of the county of ———; " and by such name may contract and be contracted with, sue and be sued, in any of the courts of this state having competent jurisdiction (*d*).

Sec. 6987. Every district shall hold in the corporate name of the district the title of lands and other property which may be acquired by said district for school district purposes. *Act December 7, 1875, sec. 53.*

Sec. 6988. No new school district shall be formed having less than thirty-five persons of scholastic age residing within the territory included in such new district, and no district now formed, shall by the formation of a new district or transfer be reduced to less than thirty-five persons of scholastic age. *Act April 8, 1887, sec. 2. See sec. 7062.*

Sec. 6989. The county court shall have the right to form new school districts or change the boundaries thereof, upon a petition of a majority of all the electors residing upon the territory of the districts to be divided (*e*).

Sec. 6990. Such territory shall have the requisite number of children or property to comply with the now existing law in such case.

Sec. 6991. In the formation of new school districts that part of territory taken off from the old district or districts, shall be held liable for a proportionate part of the indebted-

---

(*d.*) School districts are not liable for trespasses committed by their officers. *School District No. 11 v. Williams*, 38-454.

See *School District v. Bodenhamer*, 43-140; *School District v. Reeve*, 56-68.

Mandamus can only be used after judgment against a school district to force the payment of debt.

School District v. Bodenhamer, 43-140.

School property is not subject to the tax, and suit therefore, for local improvements of a public nature.

Board v. School District, 56-354.

(*e.*) This section contemplates a petition by a majority of the electors of all the districts combined, and not a majority of the electors of each district separately.

Hudspeth v. Wallis, 54-134.

ness of the former district or districts at the time of the making of said new district.

SEC. 6992. In case there be a surplus fund on hand at the time of the formation of said district, it shall be entitled to a proportionate part of said fund, the same to be ascertained and determined by the county court of the county in which said new district may be created, as in the judgment of said court may be considered right and proper. *Act April 8, 1887, sec. 3.*

APPORTIONMENT OF SCHOOL FUNDS.

SEC. 6993. The county court, immediately on receiving notice of the distributive share of school revenue apportioned by the state superintendent to each county, shall proceed to apportion to the several school districts of the county, in proportion to the number of persons between the ages of six and twenty-one years residing within the school districts, respectively, on the first Monday of July previous, the said school revenue apportioned to the county, and shall forward to the county treasurer, and to each of the directors of each district, a statement of such apportionment, carefully distinguishing the sources from which the school revenues so apportioned are derived, and the amount due each school district in the county from each separate source, and shall see that the revenues from the public school fund are invariably paid to the county and to the school districts strictly in accordance with the apportionment made to them (*f*).

In the case of *J. C. Merritt et al., v. J. H. Merritt, County Judge*, appealed from Arkansas county, the supreme court, in May, 1891, held:

"It was the duty of appellant, as county judge, on receiving notice of the amount apportioned to the county, to proceed to appropriate the same to the several districts upon whose enumeration the superintendent made the appor-

---

(*f.*) Apportionment may be compelled by mandamus, and the parents of children of schlastic age are proper parties to petition therefor.
Mattox v. Neal, 45, 121.

tionment. The duty was absolute, and in its performance the county judge had no discretion. There is no reason why a district should be kept out of its funds, for any length of time, on account of county lines, and it is the duty of the county judge to prevent it. If he fails to do his duty, its performance should be coerced."

This case clearly establishes the following principles:

1. The county judge must apportion common school funds upon the enumeration of the apportionment as made by the superintendent and upon no other. He has no right to change the enumeration and apportionment. He simply appropriates to each district the amount apportioned by the state superintendent.

2. This must be done without delay and despite changes in county lines.

3. Duties are absolute and contain no element of discretion. This principle applies to every school officer and teacher.

In view of this decision and in the change of time for making the state apportionments, I suggest that the county judge hold an adjourned term during the fourth week in August for the appropriation to districts of the funds apportioned on the first Monday in August.

The poll-tax has been distributed heretofore in two ways:

1. The amount of the *per capita* tax collected in each district of the county has been apportioned to the district in proportion to their educable children.

2. The whole amount collected in the county has been apportioned to the district in proportion to their educable children.

The latter is the proper method. The *per capita* tax is for the common schools of the county and should be apportioned upon the basis of educable children therein and not upon a narrow basis.

The following, as to the rights of the district over the funds after apportionment, are deduced from an opinion of the attorney general:

1. That the funds derived from the state, and from the *per capita* tax, and from the tax voted by the district at the annual school meeting, after they reach the county treasury and are apportioned by the county court to the school district, become the absolute property of such district for the purpose of maintaining public schools therein, subject to disbursement on the warrant of the board of directors of a separate school district.

2. That in other than separate school districts, the school directors may apply such funds to no other purpose than those directed by a majority of the electors of the district at their annual school meeting.

3. That in other than separate school districts, the electors may, at their annual meeting, fix a site for a school house, or raise money for building or purchasing a school house; *Provided*, The directors have given notice that these matters were to be submitted for consideration and action, as required by section 69 of the school law of December 7, 1875.

4. That it is within the power of the board of directors of separate school districts to apply any part of the fund belonging to such district, which has not been otherwise appropriated to the purpose of building and purchasing a school

house irrespective of the source from which such fund came, but that such power cannot be exercised by the directors of other school districts, unless they have been authorized to do so by the electors of the district at an annual school meeting. See—
> School Act of December 7, 1875.
> Lee v. Trustees of School District No. 36.
> New Jersey Equity Reports, 581.
> Mansfield's Digest, chapter 135.

SEC. 6994. Whenever a new district shall have been formed and organized, the court shall, at the next apportionment made thereafter, apportion to the new district, school revenues in proportion to the number of persons between the ages of six and twenty-one years reported by the directors of the new district; *Provided always*, The number of persons between the ages of six and twenty-one years reported in any year by the district directors of each county shall be taken as the quota of that county, and the number reported from each school district shall be taken as the quota of that district, and that the only basis on which an apportionment of the school revenue shall be made is to be the number of persons so reported each year by the district directors. *Act December 7, 1875, secs. 40, 41.*

SEC. 6995. The county examiners of the several counties shall, annually, between the tenth and twentieth days of September, transmit, verified by affidavit, to the county clerks of their respective counties a written report, showing the number of persons between the ages of six and twenty-one years residing in each school district in their respective counties, as shown by the reports of the district directors made for the same year to the county examiners, as is now required by law.

SEC. 6996. The county clerks shall, during the first terms of their respective county courts held after the reception of the reports provided for in the preceding section, lay such reports before such county courts, to be used as a guide in making the apportionment of the general school fund to the various school districts. *Act March 23, 1891..*

Sec. 6997. Any county which, by a change of county lines, or by the formation of a new county or counties, shall fail to receive the school funds which justly should be apportioned to it, from the fact of its school population being reckoned with that of the county or counties to which the said funds may be apportioned, shall be reimbursed for the loss thus incurred. Said loss shall be corrected in the first apportionment of the school revenue thereafter. *Provided*, If such correction be not made in the first apportionment thereafter, it may be made in the second (*g*).

Sec. 6998. The amounts refunded according to the provisions of section 6997 shall be deducted from the funds apportioned to the counties which were the original recipients of the erroneously apportioned revenues.

Sec. 6999. Upon the presentation of the certificate of the superintendent of public instruction of the amount or amounts due any county, by the provisions of this act, to the auditor, he shall draw his warrant on the state treasurer for said amount or amounts in favor of the treasurer of said county for the benefit of the school fund and in compliance with section 6997. *Act March 6, 1877.*

COUNTY EXAMINERS.

Sec. 7000. The county court of each county shall, at the first term thereof after each general election, appoint in each county, not divided into two judicial districts, one county examiner, and in each county divided into two judicial districts may appoint one county examiner for each district, such examiner to be of high moral character and scholastic attainments. *Act December 7, 1875, sec. 42, as amended by sec. 1, act March 20, 1883, and act March 7, 1893.*

The county examiner is one of the most important officers of the schools. He is the sentinel placed by law on the ramparts of the system. If he is capable, honest and zealous the school system will grow stronger in each county. The

---

(*g*.) See *Merritt v. School District*, 54-468.
Mandamus will lie to compel apportionment as herein provided. *Ib.*

law does not require mere moral character and mere scholastic attainment. It demands:
1. High moral character.
2. High scholastic attainments.

No one should be appointed to this office under any circumstances who is addicted in the least degree to profanity, drunkenness, gambling, licentiousness or any other demoralizing vice, or who does not believe in the existence of a Supreme Being. Teachers are not to be licensed if they have these vices, and what is forbidden to the examinee is emphatically denied to the examiner. It is a safe plan to require total abstinence in all these enumerated particulars.

As to scholastic ability the very best man in this respect should be obtained. He who is to sit in judgment upon others should be a judge. An ignorant examiner is a disgrace to the judge who appointed him and a degradation to the county.

1. The examiner must have the qualifications of an elector. He is an officer of the state—being a part of the executive department of the state. A woman may not be appointed to this position.

In *Elmore v. Overton*, 104 *Ind.*, 548, the learned judge held:

"The office of county superintendent belongs to the executive department of the state, and the statute does not confer upon the incumbent either judicial or *quasi* judicial power in the matter of licensing persons to teach in the common schools."

2. Every applicant for the position of examiner who is a teacher should present as evidences of his scholastic qualification either a license from the state superintendent or a first grade license from a competent examiner. There is no one to examine him except the state superintendent, and he can not license himself. Unless licensed by the state superintendent there is no way by which this officer may obtain a license to teach. No second or third grade teacher can measure up to the requirements of the statute which requires "high scholastic attainment."

3. Every applicant who is not a teacher should be required to show his qualifications by either a diploma from a first-class school or a license from some first-class examiner.

4. No appointments of any kind should be made as a political reward or from denominational considerations. No one should be appointed who cannot give his time to the work.

The act passed March 7, 1893, amends the preceding section in several important particulars.

SEC. 7001. Any appointments heretofore made by the county courts for the districts of such counties as are mentioned in the preceding section in which an examiner has been appointed for each district are hereby declared to be legal and valid appointments. *Act March 20, 1883, sec. 2.*

Sec. 7002. Before entering upon the duties of that office, the county examiner shall take and subscribe the oath prescribed for officers by the constitution of this state, and file such oath in the office of the county clerk. *Act March 7, 1875, sec. 43.*

Sec. 7003. All county examiners shall be required, before entering upon the duties of their offices, to stand the same examination as is required of the teachers who receive first grade licenses.

Sec. 7004. No one shall fill the offices of county examiner and school director at the same time.

Sec. 7005. The clerk of the county court in each county shall notify the superintendent of public instruction of the appointment of the county examiner in his county immediately upon his appointment, together with his name and address.

Sec. 7006. The superintendent of public instruction shall either attend in person or appoint some one duly qualified to examine such person appointed as county examiner, as to his qualifications, using the same questions as are then being used in the examination of teachers applying for first grade license.

Sec. 7007. All county examiners shall be paid such salary each year as may be fixed by the county judge of the county for which he was appointed; out of the school fund of such connty; *Provided*, Such salary shall not be greater than the amount received by the county treasurer from the tax imposed in the following section.

Sec. 7008. No county examiner shall examine any one applying to him for license as a teacher until he shall present a receipt from the county treasurer for two dollars paid by him to such treasurer to go to the credit of the county school fund. *Aet March 7, 1893, secs. 1-4.*

SCHOOL LAWS.

1. Every examiner appointed after March 7, 1893, must hold a license granted by the state superintendent of public instruction. These licenses are of two kinds, the regular state license and the examiners' license. This last instrument is based upon an examination equivalent to that upon which a first grade certificate is based, and is good for two years.

2. The office of examiner and school directors are made incompatible.

3. The examiner's fee must be paid to the county treasurer and not to the examiner. He should refuse to accept the fee at any time other than on the regular examination days, the third Thursday and Friday in June, September, December and March. The irregular days and times adopted by examiners in defiance of law and of the agreement of examiners is working great evil to the system. Some examiners set their days for public examinations a short time before the regular examination days and advertise it. Teachers from surrounding counties travel to the early examination, secure the questions and then take the regular examination in their home counties. This is wrong. The examiner has no right to change the dates of the examination. The duty is a public one and there are mutual duties and responsibilities. Each examiner owes his neighbor good faith and he is derelict when he subjects their honest labor to violence. County treasurers should refuse to be parties to the wrong. If the applicant comes at an irregular time, he should present a statement from the examiner that the examination is a private one and that the applicant has a lawful excuse for non-attendance upon the pmblic examination.

3. The intention of the statute was to fix the salary of the examiner at an amount equal to the amount paid in by the applicants for certificates, less the treasurers' commissions. It was never intended to reduce the miserable pittance already paid these officers beyond this commission.

4. This law does not repeal the law passed March 3, 1887, sec. 7025 of the digest, and which authorizes the county court to make an allowance to the examiner for express charges, postage, etc. This amount is twenty-five dollars and is an expense account, and no part of the salary. This amount, twenty-five dollars, is exclusive of the ten dollars allowed by the same act for making a report to the State Superintendent. By any fair construction the act authorized not only an amount for postage, etc., but an additional amount for the report. The first could not exceed twenty-five dollars, but was not connected with the latter allowance.

Any fee greater than two dollars is illegal. This fee is the same for either public or private examination and is to be paid for the examination and not for the certificate. It should be paid before the examination begins to the county treasurer and a receipt taken.

The examniation must be quarterly and public. The dates fixed for these quarterly examinations are the third Thursday and Friday of March June, September and December. The written questions are furnished by the state superintendent and are uniform throughout the state. The regulations as to grading of certificates are furnished to each examiner with the questions. He is positively forbidden to grant certificates without examination, or upon a partial examination, or to any one who does not reach the standards adopted by the law. The examination should be held at the school house and never in a court house. The county court should arrange for the regular use of a room in the school building.

The examiner must attend these examinations in person. He must examine upon all the branches. He can only examine at the time and place appointed. He must convince himself by evidence if the applicants are not known to him that they are of good moral character. He must exclude every person *who is given* to profanity, drunkenness, gambling, licentiousness or other demoralizing vices. Such vices may be a refusal to obey the law as to institute work or regular examination work. A positive refusal upon the part of an applicant or one holding a license to obey the school law should exclude him or take from him his license. Obedience to law is the first mark of a true teacher, and no one may claim privileges under it who refuses to obey it. He should ascertain by direct question the belief of every person as to the Supreme Being. The words "who is given to," mean either "habitual" or "habitual when opportunity affords." It requires no nice distinction to avoid extremes at this juncture. If the applicant is given to these things so as to raise a question of doubt in the mind of the examiner, the applicant should be excluded. The doubt must be resolved in favor of the schools and not in favor of the applicants. He must show a positive moral character, one emphatically marked by the absence of these vices and cannot rely upon the ordinary presumptions of innocence. He musst show himself clear or be excluded from the state's schools.

He must ascertain from the examination of each applicant under the regulations of the superintendent of public instruction not only scholarship, but competency to teach. And not only a bare competence, but a competence to teach successfully. And if the examiner is not qualified to pass upon s question he should resign his office. Every certificate granted to one who is unworthy, either mentally or morally, to receive it, is not only violation of law, but is a direct blow at the heart of our common schools. Such a certificate is an official license, not to elevate and bless, but to injure and degrade, and it may be to contaminate and curse the schools and the community. Good schools can not be taught by incompetent teachers; the moral atmosphere of the schools can not be kept pure by profane and irreverent teachers. A poor school may be a great deal worse than no school, and the state desires good teachers or none. There is no provision made in the economy of the school system for the absolutely incompetent teacher. Examiners should strike down smatterers and pretenders whenever they present themselves, no matter what may be their position in society or standing among men. They should strive to show directors and patrons that these poor teachers:

1. Plant habits of study which are hard to eradicate.

SCHOOL LAWS.   35

2. Inculcate carelessness and inattention, two fundamental educational sins.

3. Plant false ideas of facts and principles.

The examiner should carefully study the standard adopted by the state superintendent and conform thereto. This in conjunction with the one adopted by the examiner should form an invariable rule of practice in the issuance of certificates.

The state superintendent furnishes the written questions, but the examiner should supplement these by oral questions.

The oral method discloses:

(a.) Methods of teaching.
(b.) Skill and expedients.
(c.) Aptness in illustration.
(d.) Rapidity of thought.

The written plan shows:

(a.) Habits of thinking.
(b) Modes of reasoning.
(c.) Proofs of discipline.
(d.) Accuracy.
(e.) Acquaintance of principles.
(f.) Availability of knowledge.

The time to be given to each branch is suggested upon each examination sheet.

RE-EXAMINATIONS. Every examiner is required to cite for re-examination any person under contract to teach who does not sustain a good moral character, or who has not sufficient learning or ability to make him a competent teacher. He may ascertain the incompetency to teach by other means than re-examination. He may visit the schools, he may hear the directors or he may hear the parties. In all such cases, he must deal fairly, but if he is fully satisfied, he must revoke the license.

The statute permits a revocation for other than "immoral character" and "mental incompetency." The words of the statute are "for these and other adequate causes." The other adequate causes are numerous:

(a.) Refusal to conform to the law of the regulations of the state superintendent.

(b.) Refusal to conform to the regulations of directors or of the county examiner.

(c.) Refusal to obey the law as to institutes or examinations.

In all cases of this kind the teacher should have due notice and a fair hearing.

SEC. 7009. It shall be the duty of such examiner to examine and license teachers of common schools. He shall hold, quarterly, at the county seat of each county, in a suitable room to be provided by the county court, a public examination for that purpose, and shall, previous to holding such examination, give at least twenty days' notice thereof to the directors of each school district within the county, whose duty it shall be to file the original notice in their office, and post, without delay, copies of said notice in three or more of the most conspicuous places within their district. He shall conduct all examinations by written and oral questions and answers, but shall grant no certificates of qualifications except in accordance with the provisions of law respecting teachers' certificates. *Act December 7, 1875, sec. 44, as amended by act March 7, 1893, sec. 3.* See *sec. 6956.*

SEC. 7010. He shall at the time and places appointed for holding public examinations, examine in orthography, reading, penmanship, mental and written arithmetic, English grammar, modern geography, history of the United States, and in the theory and practice of teaching, and physiology and hygiene.

SEC. 7011. All persons present and applying for an examination, with the intention of teaching, the examiner, if convinced that such persons are of good moral character and are competent to teach successfully the foregoing branches, shall give such persons certificates, ranking in grades to correspond with the relative qualifications of the applicants, according to the standard adopted.

SEC. 7012. He shall not license any person to teach who is given to profanity, drunkenness, gambling, licentiousness or other demoralizing vices, or who does not believe in the existence of a Supreme Being; or shall he be required to grant private examinations.

SEC. 7013. He may cite to re-examine any person holding a license and under contract to teach any free school within his county, and on being satisfied by a re-examination, or by other means, that such person does not sustain a good moral character, or that he has not sufficient learning and ability to render him a competent teacher, he may, for these and other adequate causes, revoke the license of such person.

SEC. 7014. In case of such revocation, he shall immediately give notice thereof to such teacher and the directors, and thereby terminate the contract between the said parties, but the wages of such teacher shall be paid for the time he shall have actually taught prior to the day on which he received notice of the revocation of his license (*h*). *Act April 14, 1893.*

SEC. 7015. In addition to the branches now prescribed by law to be taught in the common schools of the state, it is made the duty of the county examiners of the several counties of this state to examine all persons applying for examination and license to teach in such schools as to their knowledge and proficiency in the method of designating and reading the survey of the lands of this state by ranges, townships and sections, and parts of sections, as surveyed, platted and designated by the government of the United States, and no such applicant shall be authorized or licensed to teach in any such school unless found upon such examination proficient in the method of designating and reading land surveys, as in this act provided.

SEC. 7016. It is made the duty and especially imposed upon all persons teaching in the public schools, to teach and impart the instructions here provided for, whenever practicable to do so, and a wilful neglect or failure to discharge the duties by this act imposed, shall be deemed sufficient cause for the revocation of license to teach. *Act February 16, 1893.*

SEC. 7017. He shall issue three grades of certificates, to be styled respectively, certificates of the first, and of the second and of the third grades. Certificates of the first

---

(*h*.) The power given the examiner to revoke license under these sections is not exclusive of the right of board of directors to terminate a contract for gross immorality and incompetency. *School District v. Maury*, 53-471.

grade shall be valid in the county for which they were issued, for two years. Those of the second grade shall be valid in the county for which they were issued, for one year. Those of the third grade shall be valid in the county, six months. But he shall not renew any certificate or grant a license without an examination of the applicant with reference thereto.

No certificate can be granted or renewed without a re examination. The examination is a personal one. The special trust is reposed in the abilities, judgment, skill and learning of the examiner, and as a consequence, the services must be personal. It is a violation of law for an examiner to adopt as his own an examination held by another; it is also unlawful to grant a certificate or renew a license without an examination, no matter what recommendations or testimonials the applicant presents. Every certificate issued by the examiner should show upon its face the degree of qualification possessed by the applicant in each of the branches named in the law. Blanks are issued by the state superintendent in conformity to law, and these should be followed by each examining officer. Certificates issued in blank should be carefully avoided.

PRIVATE EXAMINATIONS.

The examiner is not required to grant a private examination. A private examination is one held at other than the regular quarterly dates. A private examination does not mean one less difficult or less comprehensive than the public examination. Its character is exactly like the public examination in every particular, save that it is held at an irregular time. Every regulation and requirement which attaches to the stated public examination attaches to every private examination, and it is an open violation of law to conduct them on any basis other than this. Private examinations are not occasions for the examiner to do in a corner what he cannot do publicly. Examiners should never grant a private examination unless under a pressing public necessity certified to by the board of directors whose interests are affected.

SEC. 7018. He shall keep a record of the age, name, sex, post-office address and nativity of each person licensed by him to teach, and of the date and grade of his certificate, and shall include such record in his report to the state superintendent.

This record has been furnished to each examiner of the state, but the report to the superintendent has not been complied with.

SEC. 7019. He shall encourage the inhabitants to form and organize school districts, to establish public schools therein, under qualified teachers, to furnish suitable textbooks for their children and to send them to school. He shall direct the attention of teachers and school patrons to those methods of instruction that will best promote mental and moral culture, and to the most feasible and improved plan for building and ventilating school houses. He shall labor to create among the people an interest in public schools, and shall take advantage of public occasions, such as the dedication of school houses, public examinations and institutes, to impress people with the importance of educating every child, and consequently of the duty of maintaining a system of free schools established by law. He shall receive the reports of the directors, transmit an abstract of the same to the state superintendent, and transmit therewith a report of the condition and prospects of the schools under his superintendence, together with such other information and suggestions as he may deem proper to communicate.

The best place for the performance of the chief part of these duties is at the county institute. No man who can not or will not do the things required by this section should accept the office of examiner.

The interests of education in each county would be largely advanced if examiners took advantage of all public occasions to do their duty. The whole duty of an examiner is not to mark examination papers and draw the fees therefor. Neither are these duties to be separated from the duties of examination and classed as " requirements without compensation." The whole duties of the office must be taken together and the total fees collected are to be considered as full payment for the full performance of all duties. The negligence of examiners to do any one of the public acts required by this section, or to properly abstract the reports of the directors should work removal from office at once. In many cases the blame for deficient examiners' reports is cast upon the directors when the truth is that the examiners are too negligent or too lazy to do the work.

Political or religious considerations should not bias an examiner in granting certificates. If he cannot be thoroughly impartial he is not the man for the office.

The department of education looks with disfavor on private normals, held by county examiners to coach teachers for quarterly examinations. He should be absolutely disinterested in every particular, except as to merits and qualification.

SEC. 7020. He shall, annually, on or before the twentieth of September, prepare in tabular form an abstract of the reports made to him by the directors of the school districts embraced within his county, showing the number of organized districts in his county at the commencement of the year, on the first day of July preceding, the districts that have made their annual reports, the number of persons in each district between the ages of six and twenty-one years, distinguishing the sex and also the color of said persons; the number of said persons that attended school during the year; the average number of males and females of each color in daily attendance; and the number that pursued each of the studies designated to be taught in the common schools; the number of teachers of each sex employed in his county; the average wages paid per month to the teachers of each sex, according to the grade of their certificate; the whole amount paid as teachers' wages in his county; the number of pupils that studied in his county, and the several branches taught; the number of school houses erected during the year in his county, material and cost of the same; the number before erected, the material used in their construction, their condition and value; the grounds of how many inclosed; the amount of money raised by tax in each district, for what purpose raised; the amounts that have been expended, and for what purpose; the amount of revenue received by his county from the common school fund, and received for the support of schools from each of all other sources; for what purposes and in what sums the said revenues were expended, and what amounts unexpended were, at the close of the school year, in the county treasury; and shall report also the number of deaf-mutes, blind and insane in each school district in his county, under thirty years of age, their names and their post-office.

SEC. 7021. He shall number the several school districts in his county in regular order from number one upward, and shall keep in his office a record and description of each district, with the boundaries clearly defined, and also a record of such changes or alterations in the boundaries of each as shall from time to time be made.

SEC. 7022. He shall have power to appoint some suitable person to hold teachers' institutes and examine teachers in his county in case of his inability to attend such institutes and examinations. *Act December 7, 1875, secs. 45-52.*

SEC. 7023. If any county examiner shall be found incompetent, or shall be frequently neglectful of his duty, upon satisfactory proof, the county judge shall remove him from office and shall immediately appoint his successor. *Act March 11, 1881, sec. 7.*

SEC. 7024. If any county examiner shall neglect, fail or refuse to perform any of the duties required of him in section 7020, and shall not forward the abstract mentioned in said section to the superintendent of public instruction on or before the twentieth day of September of each year, he shall forfeit to the county the sum of twenty-five dollars, to be recovered as in this act provided, together with all cost, and be paid into the county treasury. *Act of March 11, 1881, sec. 11.*

SEC. 7025. Each county examiner shall make out and present to the county court of his county, at its first term after the thirtieth of June in each year, an account for expenditures for postage, county district records, or a school district map of the districts of his county, and of freight or express charges for the transmission of blanks or such other expenditures as he may have actually and unavoidably incurred, and the county court may allow the same in any sum not exceeding twenty-five dollars in any one year, including ten dollars for his report to the superintendent of public instruction.

SEC. 7026. When the county court shall have allowed the account of the county examiner as provided in the preceding section, the county clerk shall issue a warrant upon the treasurer for said claim, and upon presentation of said warrant to the county treasurer, he shall pay the same out of the common school funds in his hands belonging to the county and not yet apportioned to the several school districts. *Act March 2, 1887, secs. 2, 3.*

DECISIONS.

It has been held that a county superintendent is not entitled to an injunction to restrain one from teaching on the ground that he is teaching without a certificate of qualifications.

Perkins v. Wolf et al., 17 *Iowa*, 228.

When a statute vests a discretionary power in a county superintendent in granting licenses to teach, the judgment of the court will not be substituted for that of the officer, and mandamus will not lie to compel him to issue a license, but where he wholly fails to act on an application he may be compelled by mandamus to take action thereon.

Bailey v. Ewart, Northwestern Reporter vol. 2, N. S. vol. 2, page 1009.

High's Extraordinary Legal Remedies, secs. 24, 34, 43.

Love v. Moore, 45 *Ill.*, 12.

ANNUAL SCHOOL MEETING.

SEC. 7027. The electors of each organized school district in this state shall annually, on the third Saturday in May, at 2 o'clock p. m., hold a public meeting, to be designated "The annual school meeting of the district." *Act December 7, 1875, sec. 54, as amended by act March 11, 1881.*

SEC. 7028. All persons qualified to vote for county and state officers at the general election shall be deemed qualified electors of the school district in which they reside, and shall have the privilege of voting at all school meetings.*

SEC. 7029. The electors of every school district shall, when lawfully assembled in annual district school meeting, with not less than five electors present, have the power, by a majority of the votes cast at such meeting: First, to choose

---

*This section (7028) declares who are electors in a school meeting. Since a poll-tax receipt is necessary before voting for county and state officers, it will be necessary before voting in a school election.

a chairman ; second, to adjourn from time to time; third, to appoint, when necessary, in the absence of the directors of the district, a clerk *pro tem.;* fourth, to elect a director for the district for the next three school years, who can read and write ; fifth, to designate a site for a school house ; sixth, to determine the length of time during which a school shall be taught more than three months in a year; seventh, to determine what amount of money shall be raised by tax on the taxable property of the district, sufficient, with the public school revenues apportioned to the district, to defray the expenses of a school for three months, or for any greater length of time they may decide to have a school taught during the year; *Provided,* No tax for purposes aforesaid greater than one-half of one per cent. on the assessed value of the taxable property of the district shall be levied ; *And provided, further,* They may, if sufficient revenue cannot be raised to sustain a school for three months in any one year, determine by ballot that no school shall be taught during such year, in which case the revenue belonging to such district shall remain in the treasury to the credit of such school district ; eighth, to repeal or modify their proceedings from time to time (*i*).

The powers of the electors as enumerated herein when legally exercised are final, and absolutely determine the matters named in the enumeration. But should the electors presume to act upon other matters not herein enumerated their action would be advisory and not mandatory. For instance ; should the electors vote upon the teacher to be employed, or the time when the school should begin, or the wages to be paid the teacher, their action would not preclude the directors from acting differently. All such matters are given into the hands of the directors, and while the electors may advise they may not direct upon any matter not enumerated in the law.

The enumerated powers of the electors are :

1. To choose a chairman. Failure to choose a chairman does not invalidate the election by ballot held by judges and clerks under the law.

(*i.*) Directors have no power to build a school house with funds of the district unless authorized to do so at the annual school meeting, and a contract made for such purpose under authority conferred by a special meeting held in June, is void. *Fluty v. School District,* 49–94.

2. To adjourn from time to time. If there is any business that cannot be attended to at the annual school meeting an adjourned meeting or meetings should be provided for at the annual meeting. Otherwise it must wait the next regular annual meeting.

3. To appoint a clerk.

4. To elect a director for the district for the next three school years who can read and write. Electors have no more right to elect a director who cannot read and write than they have to elect a director who lives in another state or who is not an elector; and such an election confers no right to hold the office. Section 7040 authorizes the electors to elect a director to fill vacancies, and this should be done at the same time that the director is chosen who is to serve three years. To distinguish between the director who is to serve three years and the one who is to fill the vacancy the tickets in such cases should indicate in addition to the men's names the length of term for which the director is to serve. The words "regular term," "two years," and "one year," are a sufficient marking. The elector has the right not only to vote for any eligible person for director, but in cases where vacancies are to be filled to vote for the man and the place he is to fill or the time he is to serve. Votes cast for the same person but for different times must be counted separately.

5. To designate a site for a school house. This action may be taken at the annual meeting, or at an adjourned meeting of the annual meeting. No special meeting may be called to do this or any other act enumerated in the section except the election of a director to fill a vacancy. Before the site may be lawfully designated at such annual meeting the notice required by section 7053 must have been given.

6. To determine the length of time during which a school shall be taught more than three months in a year. This has given rise to some confusion of thought and action. Electors seem to think that unless they have voted affirmatively for an extended term that three months is the limit of the school term. This is not the case. The object for which taxes are levied is to maintain schools. This is affirmed in both constitution and law. Now, if the money apportioned to the district from the state and from the *per capita* tax is sufficient to maintain a school for more than three months it is the duty of the directors, without any affirmative action on the part of the electors, to maintain the school. The whole object of the statute was to prevent directors from incurring debt, and to permit the electors to provide money by local tax for an extended term, provided such tax were needed. And if the electors, without specifically voting for an extended term, vote such a local tax upon themselves as will maintain an extended term, it is tantamount to saying they voted to extend the school. It cannot be argued that men will levy a tax upon themselves to remain idle in the treasury. Directors may lawfully maintain a school to the limit of the funds on hand or that will be on hand by operation of law during the year. They cannot go beyond this. Directors are required to maintain a school for three months at least, and if the

funds are not sufficient to defray all expenses of such school a lesser term may not be contracted for unless the electors have either failed to vote by ballot that no school shall be taught that year, or have voted down the proposition of no school. In such cases the only alternative for the directors is to maintain the school for the longest time consistent with the means on hand. Where directors have money sufficient to maintain a three months' school any shorter term is unlawful. No term of school of three months should be divided. It should go on continuously to the end.

7. To determine what amount of money shall be raised by taxation to defray the expenses of a school for three months or for any greater length of time. If this amount is not determined by the *viva voce* vote of the electors in the annual meeting, but a local tax is levied nevertheless by ballot at the election following the mass meeting, the local tax must be taken as the determination of this question, and the directors are thereby authorized to maintain the school for three months or for such longer term as the tax levied will justify. If the tax levied is specifically devoted to building, repairs, or any other object, it may not be appropriated to the payment of teachers' salaries.

8. To repeal and modify their proceedings. The annual meeting, or mass meeting, of the electors should be attended by all the electors. The account of the directors should be investigated by committee or by the whole body; questions affecting the interest of the district should be discussed calmly and dispassionately; the good of the school should govern every citizen who attends the meeting. After the mass meeting the election should begin by ballot and proceed regularly under the law. Good sense, good order and patriotism should characterize every mass meeting of citizens.

Besides these powers, the electors are authorized by section 7042, to direct the sale or exchange of the site or school house; and by section 7065, to direct the use of the school house with reference to private schools; and by section 7050 to direct the proceedings in all actions and suits at law brought for or against the district, if they elect to do so.

DECISIONS.

Where a meeting of a school district is held for a special purpose, all that is necessary in the form of the notice is that it should be so expressed as that the inhabitants of the district may fairly understand the purpose for which they are convened.

School District v. Blakeslee, 13 *Conn.*, 227.
Weeks v. Batchelder, 41 *Vt.*, 317.
Moore v. Beattie, 33 *Vt.*, 219.
Bartlett v. Kinsley, 15 *Conn.*, 227.

Reasonable time for opening meeting after convening.
School District v. Blakeslee, 13 *Conn.*, 227.

Money for school purposes may be voted at an adjourned meeting in New Jersey.

State v. Lewis, 35 *N. J. L.,* 377.

Where it appears that a site for a school house has been chosen, it will not be invalidated because the clerk has made irregularitties or omissions in describing the site selected.

Merritt v. Farris, 22 *Ill.,* 303.

Record of the school meeting, how attacked and the presumptions of law flowing from it.

School District v. Blakeslee, 13 *Conn.,* 227.

Bartlett v. Kinsley, 15 *Conn.,* 327.

School District v. Atherton, 12 *Met.* (*Mass.*), 105.

As to posting of notices.

Fletcher v. Lincolnville, 20 *Me.,* 439.

SEC. 7030. The annual district election shall be held by the school directors as judges, who shall have power to appoint two clerks; and if any of the directors should not attend, the assembled voters may choose judges in the place of those not attending, and the judges and clerks shall take the oath prescribed by the general election law.

SEC. 7031. The ballot of the voter shall, in addition to the names of the persons voted for as directors, have written or printed on it the words " for tax," or " against tax," and also the amount of tax the voter desires levied.

SEC. 7032. When the polls are closed (*j*) the judges shall proceed to count the votes, ascertain the result and make return thereof to the county court, showing the number of votes cast for each person voted for for school director, also the number cast for and against tax, and the number of votes cast for each amount or rate of tax voted for (*k*); such return, together with the ballots, shall be sealed up and delivered by one of the judges to the county clerk, at least

(*j.*) As to time for opening and closing the polls, see *Holland v. Davies,* 36-446.

(*k.*) Unless the judges make return of the election or vote to the county court, it can not levy the tax. *Hodgkin v. Fry,* 33-716. The omission of the judges to state in their return the number of votes cast for and against the proposed tax will not defeat a levy adopted by the meeting. *Holland v. Davies,* 36-446; *Staley v. Leomans,* 53-428. As to other irregularities, see *Holland v. Davies, supra,* and *Rogers v. Kerr,* 42-100.

ten days before the meeting of the county court for levying taxes.

SEC. 7033. The county court, at its said meeting for levying taxes, shall open the return and ascertain whether a majority of the votes cast be for tax; and if a tax has been voted, then the court shall determine the amount of taxes voted by taking the largest amount or rate of taxation voted for by a majority of the voters, which shall be levied and collected by the district so voting; and if no rate shall have received such majority, then all the votes cast for the highest rate shall be counted for the next highest, and so on, till some rate voted shall receive a majority of all the votes cast. *Act December 7, 1875, secs. 55 and 56, as amended by act April 10, 1893, sec. 4.*

SEC. 7034. All taxes voted for school purposes by any school district shall be levied by the county court at the same time the county taxes are levied, and shall be collected in the same manner as the county taxes are collected, at the same time and by the same person, and be paid into the county treasury, there to be kept subject to disbursement on the warrant of the school directors; *Provided*, No tax for the purposes aforesaid greater than one-half of one per cent. on the assessed value of the taxable property of the district shall be levied, which shall be done by ballot (*l*). *Act December 7, 1875, sec. 41.*

SCHOOL DIRECTORS.

SEC. 7035. At the annual school meeting, held on the third Saturday in May, there shall be elected, by the legal voters in each school-district, a director, who shall hold his office for the term of three years, and until his successor

---

(*l*.) The county court has no power to levy a school tax independent of action on the part of the electors of each school district for which the tax is levied; it can only cause to be placed on the tax-books and collected such rates as are reported from the districts. An excessive levy vitiates the whole tax. *Worthen v. Badgett*, 32-496. See *Ry. v. Parks, Ib.*, 131; *Rogers v. Kerr*, 42-100.

shall have been elected and have qualified. *Provided,* At the first annual school meeting of the district after the passage of this act, three school directors shall be elected, to hold office one, two and three years, respectively; *Provided, further,* When a new school district shall have been formed under the provisions of this act, three directors shall be immediately elected by the electors of the new district, and shall hold their office for one, two and three years, respectively, and until their successors are elected and qualified as herein provided for. *Act December 7, 1875, sec. 57, as amended by act March 11, 1881, sec. 2, and act January 30, 1889.*

SEC. 7036. The judges of any school election of this state for school directors shall within five days after said election give to the said elected director a certificate of his election, who shall within ten days thereafter take the oath of office prescribed for directors, and file the same, together with his certificate of election, with the county clerk of his county, and enter at once upon the duties of his office (*m*). *Act January 30, 1889.*

SEC. 7037. An old director shall, upon application of an incoming director, administer to him the oath of office. *Act March 11, 1881, sec. 5.*

SEC. 7038. Any person who shall have been elected or appointed a director, and shall neglect or refuse to qualify and serve as such, shall forfeit to his district the sum of ten dollars, which may be recovered by action against him at the instance of any elector in the district, and which, when collected, shall be paid into the county treasury by the officer before whom the action was maintained, and added, by the treasurer, to the school fund revenues appropriated to the district.

(*m.*) For decision under this section before amended to read as now, see *School District v. Bennett,* 52-511. It is not sufficient to take the oath orally. *School District v. Bennett,* 52-428.

SEC. 7039. Any director who shall neglect or fail to perform any duties of his office shall forfeit to his district the sum of twenty-five dollars, to be recovered as directed in the preceding section, and to add in like manner to the school fund revenues apportioned to his district.

This section gives a penalty for a violation of any duty enjoined upon the directors, and may be recovered at the instance of any elector.

SEC. 7040. If the office of any director in a district becomes vacant, the electors of said district shall, in a district meeting assembled, within fifteen days after the occurrence of such vacancy, elect a director to serve the remainder of the unexpired term; but if the district in which such vacancy occurs neglects or fail to elect a director to fill such vacancy, then the county court shall appoint from the electors of said district a director to serve the remainder of the term.

From section 7036 it is plain that the last day upon which the newly-elected director may take the oath of office may be fifteen days from the third Saturday in May. In case no director is elected the vacancy named in this section, would begin on the fifteenth day after the third Saturday in May, and the electors will have the right within fifteen days, or within thirty days after the annual meeting to elect a director for a vacancy caused by a failure to elect at the proper time. For a vacancy caused by death, resignation or otherwise, the electors have fifteen days from the date of such death, resignation or other occurrence which caused the vacancy to fill the same.

SEC. 7041. The said board shall make provisions for establishing separate schools for white and colored children and youths (*n*), and shall adopt such other measures as they may judge expedient for carrying the free school system into effectual and uniform operation throughout the state,

---

(*n*.) It is the duty of directors to provide equal school facilities for blacks and whites. *Maddox v. Neal*, 45-121. The board of directors cannot claim to apportion the school funds and limit the school terms to each class according to its scholastic population. *Ib.*

S—4

and providing, as nearly as possible, for the education of every youth (*o*).

The duty of establishing separate schools for both races is mandatory. If there are eleven or more black children, or eleven or more white children, they must have a school. Ten black children or a less number, or ten white children or less should be transferred to an adjoining district under the provisions of the act approved April 3, 1891. See sec. 7062.

In the case of *Maddox et al. v. Neal et al., Ark. Rep.*, 121, the supreme court of this state says: "A wide range of discretion is vested in these boards by the statute in the matter of the government and details of conducting of the common schools, but in the nature of things, there is a limit to this discretion. Some positive and imperative duties are imposed upon them about which they have no discretion. The first and most important duty of the board is to make provisions for establishing schools. When the funds are provided, and the directors are not otherwise instructed by the school meeting of the district, the duty to provide a school for at least three months is mandatory, and the duty to establish separate schools for the whites and blacks is also incumbent on them. All the provisions of the law in relation to schools, in conformity to the constitutional mandate, are general, and the system, as far as the statute can make it, is uniform. No duty is imposed upon or discretion given to the directors about schools for one race that is not applicable to the other. It is the clear intention of the constitution and statutes alike to place the means of education within the reach of every youth. Education at the public expense has become a legal right extended by the laws to all the people alike. No discrimination on account of nationality, caste or other distinction has been attempted by the law-making powers. The boards of directors are only the agents, the trustees appointed to carry out the system provided for. Their powers are no greater than the authority conferred by legislation. They can do nothing they are not expressly authorized to do, or which does not grow out of their expressed powers. * * * The opportunity of instruction in public schools, given by the statute to all the youths of the state, is in obedience, as we have seen, to special command of the constitution, and it is obvious that a board of directors can have no discretionary power to single out part of the children by the arbitrary standard of color, and deprive them of the benefits of the school privilege. To hold otherwise would be to set the discretion of the directors above all law."

SEC. 7042. The directors shall have charge of the school affairs and of the school educational interests of their dis-

---

(*o*.) In the discharge of their duties, in this section prescribed, the board has discretion, but when it fails to perform its duties *mandamus* will lie to compel it to do so. *Maddox v. Neal*, 45-121.

trict, and shall have the care and custody of the school houses and grounds, the books, records, papers and other property belonging to the district, and shall carefully preserve the same, preventing waste and damage; and shall purchase or lease, in the corporate name of the district, such school-house site as may be designated by a majority of the legal voters at the district meeting; shall hire, purchase or build a school house with funds provided by the district for that purpose; and may sell or exchange such site or school house, when so directed by a majority of the electors of any legal meeting of the district (*p*).

In general, school property is to be used for the purposes of education. It appears that the legislature has not inhibited the directors from permitting the school house to be used temporarily and occasionally for other purposes. In Indiana it has been held that a school house may be used for township purposes.

Trustees v. Osborne, 9 *Ind.*, 458

The school house may be used for all lawful school district meetings of the electors or directors.

In Iowa it has been held that the electors may direct the use of school houses for religious purposes. So in Ohio and Vermont.

Chapin v. Hill, 24 *Vt.*, 528.
Weir v. Day, Supreme Court of Ohio, 1879.
Central Law Journal, Vol. 9, 398.
Davis v. Boget, 50 *Ia.*, 194.

It has been held that the words, "to direct the sale or other disposition to be made of any school house," conferred the power on the electors to vote upon the question as to whether the school house should be used for religious purposes.

Townshend v. Heagan et al., 35 *Iowa*, 194.

Section 7042 by implication vests the power of directing the sale or exchange of the site or the school house in the electors alone. It is doubtful whether this authority may be so expanded as to authorize them to direct the temporary occasional use of the house. This authority appears to be vested by our statutes in the discretion of the directors alone.

In Illinois it has been held that the temporary use of a school house is not

---

(*p.*) Two members of the boards may bind the district at a contract, made at a meeting at which the third was present or had notice; but no contract can be made except at a meeting of which all had notice. *School District v. Bennett*, 52-511.

See *Widner v. State*, 49-172.

forbidden by the constitution of that state. Nor is it forbidden by the constitution of Arkansas.

In *Nichols v. School Directors, Superior Court of Illinois*, November 10, 1879, it was held that an incidental use of a school house for religious purposes, not interfering with school purposes, is not in any reasonable sense inconsistent with the faithful application of the property to school purposes. Religion and religious worship are not so placed under the ban of the constitution that they may not be allowed to become the recipient of any incidental benefit from the authorities of the state.

In Connecticut, however, it was held that a single tax-payer might prevent the use of the school property for religious purposes by simply objecting thereto, and that he was entitled to an injunction to inforce his right.

Schofield v. Eighth School Dist., 27 *Conn.*, 499.

The legislature of Connecticut afterwards enacted a law placing the right to direct the use of school property in a two-thirds vote of the electors

. Section 7065 authorizes the directors to permit the use of the school house by a private school unless otherwise directed by a majority of the legal voters of the district. This enlargement of the power of the electors, as set out in section 7029 and in 7042, as to directing the sale or exchange of the site or school house, must be considered in construing these sections; and the exercise of the enlarged power must be controlled by the provisions of section 7029, that is, the electors may act upon these questions at the annual meeting or an adjournment thereof.

It is evident that the respective powers and rights of directors and electors are not clear. The general principle is that the whole matter is left to the sound discretion of the directors, subject to a controlling direction on the part of the electors as to a private school.

SEC. 7043. They shall hire for and in the name of the district, such teachers as have been licensed according to law, and shall make with such teachers a written contract, specifying the time for which the teacher is to be employed, the wages to be paid per month and any other agreement entered into by the contracting parties, and shall furnish the teachers with a duplicate of such contract, and keep the original; and they shall employ no person to teach in any common school of their district unless such person shall hold, at the time of commencing his school, a certificate and license to teach, granted by the county examiner or state superintendent.

The right to select a teacher, fix his salary, and the time for the opening of the school are matters which belong exclusively to the directors. The electors have no right to direct upon any question connected with the teaching of the school, save the single one of extending the term of the school.

Directors cannot make a legal contract with a teacher who has no licenses. This negatives the right to contract with a principal teacher who is licensed for an amount of money to be paid him, out of which he is to pay the salaries of unlicensed assistants.

Every teacher, whether as principal or assistant, must be selected by the board of directors; every such person must have a license from the county examiner or state superintendent, and every such person must have a written contract. County treasurers are warranted to demand the contract of every teacher or assistant who presents a warrant for the payment of wages from the public school funds. If the warrant shows that its holder is principal, and that the amount specified on its face is for the payment of the wages of assistants, or if it is proven to the treasurer that such is the case, he should refuse to pay the same as a violation of sections 7051 and of 7043. The treasurer may also refuse to pay the warrant of any teacher who has not been licensed. See section 7052. The words, "properly drawn" in this section refer back to the inhibitions of section 7043, and forward to the positive inhibition of section 7071, and the treasurer should exercise the greatest caution in the matter of paying these doubtful warrants.

The acts of school directors are corporate acts. To bind the district it is necessary for them to act at a regular meeting, or a called meeting, of which, notice was given to each director. At such meetings the act of a majority of the board is the act of the whole board.

CONTRACTS.

A board of school directors empowered by statute without any limitation to employ a superintendent of schools may make a contract for a superintendent for a term beginning after some members of the board go out of office.

Gates v. School District of Fort Smith, 53 *Ark.*, 468.

Davis v. School District, 81 *Mich.*, 214.

This decision applies to all teachers employed in the schools as well as to the superintendent.

The following opinion of the attorney general contains the law upon this point:

The office of school director is a very important one—more important than is generally considered by the people. The best men in the district should be selected for this responsible position. The progress and development of our various resources depends, in a great measure, upon the efficiency of school directors. Although the lowest of elective officers, yet it is equal to the highest in its influence in advancing the prosperity of the state.

School directors have charge of the educational interests of their respective districts; have the care and custody of school houses, grounds, books, records, papers, etc.; they shall purchase or lease school-house site designated by the legal voters; they shall hire, purchase or build a school house with funds provided for that purpose; they shall hire and contract with teachers; they shall adopt a series of text-books to be used in the district school; they shall furnish teachers with a register; they shall visit the schools and submit to the district an an estimate of the expenses of said district; draw warrants on the treasurer; make the enumeration and enrollment report between the 1st and 10th of September, and make settlements with the county treasurer, etc.

For the purpose of carrying out the above-mentioned duties with wisdom and discretion, each district has three school directors. These directors constitute an educational board, and should meet and transact all business of the district as a board. The first business of a school board, composed of continuing and newly elected members, is to organize by electing a president and secretary. Directors are possessed of specially defined powers, and should exercise no others, and cannot do so legally. In the transaction of all business pertaining to the district, all members of the board must meet together, or have notice to meet. The action of a majority of the school board will not bind the district when one of the directors had no notice of the meeting and did not participate in it. (4 *Nebr.*, 254.) The district has a right to the wisdom, experience and judgment of each director, and a majority of the directors cannot legally bind the district unless each member of the board has had due and timely notice of said meeting. A contract by two of the members of the board, when all have had notice, is legal and binding on the district. When a board is by statute made a body corporate, individual members acting separately, although a majority, cannot contract a debt or draw a warrant for its payment.

22 *Ohio*, 144; 27 *Kan.*, 129.

This additional opinion contains another principle.

Sir—In answer to your inquiries I have the honor to say that, in my opinion, section 7043 applies as well to special, or single school districts, as to ordinary common school districts.

I am also of the opinion that it applies to the superintendent of schools in such special districts, provided he is to act as a teacher, otherwise not.

I am also of opinion that said section is mandatory upon the directors, but I do not believe, or mean to be understood as saying, that a verbal contract made with a qualified teacher would be void because not in writing.

The contracts made by a board of directors are good though it should turn out that the directors are disqualified to hold office. They are *de facto* officers.

Sec. 7044. The term "month," wherever it occurs in any section of this act, shall be construed to mean twenty days, or four weeks of five days each. *Act December 7, 1875, secs 58–62.*

SEC. 7045. The directors of school districts, other than special school districts, may expend annually, out of the common school fund, not more than twenty-five dollars during any one year for any school under their control for maps, charts, globes, dictionaries and other apparatus necessary to the progress of the school; *Provided*, Said maps, charts, globes, dictionaries and other apparatus meets the approval of the state superintendent, in price and merit. *Act February 16, 1893.*

SEC. 7046. The directors of each school district in this state shall adopt and caused to be used in the public schools, in their respective districts, one series of text-books in each branch or science taught in the public schools of their respective districts, and no change in these books shall be made for a period of three years, unless it be by a petition of a majority of the voters of the district desiring the change. *Act March 11, 1881, sec. 2.*

See section 6975 and comments and opinion therein set out. The penalty for failure to perform the duties imposed by this act is a fine of not less than ten nor more than fifty dollars. See *sec.* 7070.

SEC. 7047. They shall procure from the county examiner, and furnish the teacher at the commencement of the term, a register for his school, and require the said teacher to report, in said register, at the close of the school term, the number of days of the said term, the name and age of each pupil, the date on which each entered the school, the separate days on which each attended, the whole number of days each attended, the studies each pursued, the total number of days all pupils attended, the average daily attendance and the number of visits received from the directors during the said term. *Act December 7, 1875, sec. 63.*

The keeping of this register according to all its requirements, perfected and complete, is compulsory upon the teacher, and he can not draw his last month's wages until this duty is performed. See *sec.* 7076.

SEC. 7048. They shall visit the schools at least once each

term, and encourage the pupils in their studies, and give such advice to the teacher as may be for the benefit of teacher and pupils.

SEC. 7049. They shall submit to the district, at the annual meeting, an estimate of the expenses of the district for that year, including the expenses of a school for the term of three months for the next year, after deducting the probable amount of school moneys to be apportioned to the district for that school year, and shall also submit an estimate of the expenses per month of continuing the school beyond the term of three months, and of whatever else may be necessary for the comfort and advancement of the said school.

The following is the blank prescribed to meet the requirements of this section:

SCHOOL LAWS. 57

DIRECTORS' ESTIMATE OF DISTRICT EXPENSES.

Electors of School District No.............., County of ....State of Arkansas:

We respectively submit the following as our estimate of the expenses of the public schools in this district for the term of three months during the present scholastic year, beginning the first of last July, and of the expenses per month of continuing the schools longer than three months:

	AMOUNT NECESSARY.	
For teachers' salaries		
For purchase or lease of sites		
For purchase, erection or hire of houses..........................		
For repairs of houses and grounds..		
For fuel and incidental expenses...........................		
For furniture, apparatus, light, etc............		
For other purposes		
Total..........		
Amount we will probably receive from the state apportionment....		
Remainder to be raised by a district tax		
Expense for continuing the schools............... .... longer than three months, at......... ... . dollars per month..........		
Total amount to be raised by district tax..		

The electors are respectively asked to vote a tax of............ mills to meet the expenses of the above estimate.

.... ⎫
.... ⎬ *Directors.*
.... ⎭

It will be seen that there are several items of expense. Should the directors fill each blank, thus recommending a tax for each item of expense, and should the electors vote the rate of tax suggested, or any other rate, without expressly negativing an item recommended, then the tax voted must be held to be voted in strict compliance with the estimate; and the estimate should be returned with the poll books to the county clerk so that the county judge in making his levy may levy to suit the vote and the estimate which is the basis of the vote. The tax levied and the items of the estimate should be certified by the clerk to the treasurer. The treasurer should distribute the tax when collected to the various purposes named in the estimate, opening an account with each special item, the only index to the purpose for which the tax was levied. Should the tax collected be more or less than the amount of the estimate, then each item of the estimate must be increased or decreased in proportion. It must never be forgotten that the estimate submitted by the directors is a necessary part of the election, and is the only source from which the intention of the electors as to the purpose of the tax is to be gathered, except the ballots. If the ballots declare "for five mills," with no accompanying words, then the court in levying the tax is relegated to the estimate for the purpose of the tax; and if the estimate distributes the expense by items, then the necessary and only inference is that the tax was voted for the express purpose of meeting the estimate. If the ballots declare " for tax " and the estimate is not itemized, but massed under the general words "for common school purposes" or "for general purposes" or any other language which intimates generality of purpose, or should the ballots themselves declare this generality, then the necessary and only legal inference is that the tax was to be levied for general purposes, and should be so levied by the court. And in every case where the vote is so generalized the directors are empowered to distribute the tax so levied and collected for any and every necessary school purpose except building a house. No house can be built under the general authority " for general purposes," although any other necessary expense may be met that way. The treasurer is always authorized to pay the warrants of a board of directors for any purpose save building where the levy of the court or the vote of the electors was " for general purposes " or other general language.

But if the estimate submitted to the electors is limited by the words " for teachers' salaries," and the ballots are simply " for tax," then the levy is special, and the tax when collected must be distributed "for teachers' salaries alone." It is better for every interest of the district that the ballots declare " for general school purposes." This will vest a discretion in the directors, and will enable them to meet the demands of the school at any time. These comments have force only as they concern the "local tax." The funds received from the state apportionment and from the *per capita* tax are not under the control of the electors, save that where they are not sufficient to maintain a three months' school the electors may direct them to remain in the treasury.

Such funds, with the exception named are under the control of the directors alone, and must be used to maintain free schools. In doing this the directors may use them for paying the salaries of teachers and all necessary expenses incident thereto. It is difficult to draw the line between necessary and unnecessary expenses, and where there are grave doubts as to this the directors should not incur the expense. Several supreme courts have decided that "maps, globes, charts and other illustrative appliances," are not necessary, and directors are relieved from deciding this question. The legislature wisely permits them to buy these things from an approved list to the amount of twenty-five dollars each year.

But " repair of house " when imperative and which cannot be delayed to the annual meeting of the electors, fuel, stoves, blackboards, buckets, dippers, crayons and erasers, are necessary incidents to the life of a school and are proper charges upon the state and *per capita* apportionment. Seats are necessary, of course, but as they are a part of the building itself they must be furnished by a like process; a special tax must be levied. The words " for building purposes " will authorize the directors not only to build but to furnish with seats. The only trouble that can arise is where there is an entire absence of seats and a positive refusal on the part of the electors to provide a tax for their purchase. In that case no school can be supported. The law expressly empowers the directors "to hire, purchase or build a school house, with funds provided by the district for that purpose." and no other funds can be used. It follows then that the local tax is absolutely necessary before a house may be rented, built, purchased or furnished. The words " for general purposes " in the voting of a local tax will authorize the use of the tax for hiring or furnishing; but to purchase or build there must be a vote for this specific purpose.

SEC. 7050. They shall, in all suits and actions at law brought by or against their district, appear for and in behalf of said district. *Provided,* They shall have no other directions or instructions by a lawful meeting of the electors of their district.

SEC. 7051. They shall draw orders on the treasurer of the county for the payment of wages due teachers, or for any lawful purpose, and they shall state in every such order the services or consideration for which the order is drawn, and the name of the person rendering such service; but they shall not draw any order on the county treasurer for the payment of the wages of any teacher not licensed (*q*).

SEC. 7052. When the warrant of any board of directors, properly drawn, is presented to the treasurer of the proper county, he shall pay the same out of any funds in his hands for that purpose belonging to the district specified in said warrant (*r*). See *sec. 7043*.

SEC. 7053. The directors shall give notice of each annual

(*q.*) School warrants may be issued by two directors. *Crain v. State*, 45-450.

(*r.*) Statutes of limitation run against school warrants. *School District v. Cromer*, 52-454; *School District v. Reeve*, 56-68.

Effect of warrants drawn in lieu of destroyed or lost warrants, see *School District v. Cromer*, 52-454.

meeting, by posting notices thereof, at least fifteen days previous to such meeting, in three or more conspicuous places within the district (*s*); but it shall not be lawful for a district, at any annual meeting, to fix a site for a schoolhouse, or to raise money for building or purchasing a schoolhouse, unless the directors shall have particularly set forth in the previous notice given of such meeting that these matters were to be submitted for their consideration and action (*t*).

SEC. 7054. One of the directors shall act as clerk at all district meetings, shall keep a record of the proceedings thereof in a book provided for that purpose, or, if absent, shall transcribe into said book the minutes kept by the clerk *pro tempore*, and signed by the chairman, as so much of the authenticated records of the district; and he shall enter on the said book copies of all his reports to the county clerk and the county examiner.

SEC. 7055. He shall keep, in a book provided for that purpose, the accounts of the district, by debits and credits, including the accounts with the county treasurer, and shall present the same to each annual meeting, showing the current expenses for the year, for school-houses, out-buildings, fences with which to inclose a school-house site, for stoves, wood, maps, charts, blackboards, a dictionary, and other necessaries for a school, and stating the number of days the directors have been necessarily employed in the performance of their duties as directors; the date of each order drawn by them on the county treasurer, and for what services or con-

---

(*s*.) It is the duty of the directors to designate the place of the annual meeting, and notice of the time and place is essential to the validity of a tax voted at such meeting. But the statute designates the time, and all are bound to take notice of it. If notice of the place be given, the meeting will be legal, though the time be not specified in the notice. *Hodgkin v. Fry*, 33-716. A notice given by two of the directors is sufficient. *Holland v. Davies*, 36-446; *Davies v. Holland*, 43-425.

(*t*.) See *Fluty v. School District*, 49-94.

sideration, for what amounts and in whose favor, exhibiting vouchers therefor; a statement of the indebtedness of the district, and also of the surplus moneys, if any, in the county treasury belonging to the district at the commencement of the year; the amount of taxes levied on the district for school purposes within the year; the different purposes for which said taxes were levied, and the amount levied for each purpose. If, on examination, the report be found correct, the chairman of the meeting shall approve the same, and order that it be filed with the records of the district.

SEC. 7056. The directors shall, within ten days after any school meeting, report to the clerk of the county so much of the proceedings of said meeting as pertains to the election of officers; and they shall, on or before the first day of October in each year, furnish to the clerk so much of the copy of their record, attested by the chairman of the meeting, as shows the amount of money voted to be raised by the district, for school purposes, at the annual meeting.

SEC. 7057. They shall, annually, between the first and tenth days of September, transmit, verified by their affidavit, to the county examiner, a written report, in proper form, of the name of their county; of the number of their district; the names and ages of all persons, between the ages of six and twenty-one years, residing in their district on the first day of September; the number of males and females respectively, of each color, that attended the common schools during the last school year; the average number of each sex that attended daily; the number that pursued each of the studies designated to be taught in the common schools of this state; the number of times the school was visited each term by the directors; the number of days the school was taught during the year by a licensed teacher; the name of each teacher; the grade of his certificate; the wages paid each teacher per month, and the whole amount of wages paid teachers during the year. They shall include in their report the amount of taxes voted by the district during the last school year, for what purpose voted, and the amount voted for each purpose; the amount drawn from the county treasurer for each purpose for which money was raised by district tax the previous year; the amount of revenues received from the common school fund, and the amount received from each of the various other sources from which school revenues are derived; the amount of each kind of revenue remaining in the county treasury and subject to the order of the district; the number of school houses erected during the year, and the cost and material of each; the number, the material, the condition and the value of those before erected, and the value of all other property belonging to the district; the condition of the school-house grounds, and whether the said grounds are enclosed; also, name, age and post-office of deaf, dumb, blind and insane in each district, including all who are blind or deaf, or to such an extent as not to be educated in common schools; and they shall record the said report in the proper place in the district book in which the current record of the proceedings of the district is kept.

SEC. 7058. If the directors of any district fail or neglect to make a report of the enumeration, statistics and finances of their district at the time and in the manner prescribed in the preceding section, the said directors, in addition to their forfeiture for neglect of duty, shall severally be liable for any damages, including the costs of the suit, that the district may sustain by reason of losing the school revenues that would otherwise have been apportioned to them.

SEC. 7059. They shall, at the close of the school year, settle with the county treasurer, and ascertain what moneys, if any, to which their district may be entitled, and the amounts, severally, thereof that are in the county treasury and subject to be drawn by their district. *Ib.*, *secs. 64-75.*

SEC. 7060. The directors of any school district may, at

the instance of the teacher, suspend from the school any pupil for gross immorality, refractory conduct or insubordination, or for infectious disease. *Provided*, Such suspension shall not extend beyond the current term.

Directors should remember that the right to attend school grows out of *bona fide* residence and not from an enumeration in a district or the payment of taxes. When a man moves into a district with the intention of making it his permanent residence, he acquires the right to send to the public schools at once. The directors are to decide from all the circumstances, whether the residence is permanent or temporary. If temporary no free school privileges obtain.

It will be seen that the power to suspend is lodged with the directors. The teacher has no authority to perform this act of discipline upon his own motion. He must report the infraction of discipline to the board of directors, who are alone authorized to act.

DECISIONS.

The general school committee of a town has power to exclude therefrom a child of immoral or licentious character though such character be not manifested by any acts in the school room. The learned judge reasoned as follows : " It seems to be admitted, if not, it could hardly be questioned, that for misconduct in school, for disobedience to its reasonable regulations, a pupil may be excluded. Why so? There is no express provision in the law (as it then was) authorizing such exclusion; it results by necessary implication, from the provision of law requiring good discipline. It proves that the right to attend school is not absolute, but one to be enjoyed by all on reasonable conditions."

Trustees v. People, 87 *Illinois*, 303.
Ruleson v. Post, 79 *Ill.*, 567.
Morrow v. Wood, 36 *Wis.*, 59.
Sherman v. Charleston, 8 *Cush.*, 160.
Peck v. Smith, 41 *Conn.*, 442.

It is undoubtedly true that trustees or committees have the power, and it is their duty to dismiss or exclude a pupil from their school when, in their judgment, it is necessary for the good order and proper government of the school so to do.

Stephenson v. Hall, 14 *Barb.*, 222.

They may do so to prevent a pupil from bringing contagion into a school.

Spear v. Cummins, 23 *Pick.*, 225.

The school authorities have a right to exclude from their grounds or buildings anyone who enters therein to disturb the peace or interfere with the legitimate exercises of the school.

Hughes v. Goodell, 3 *Pittsb., L. J.*, 264.

Whatsoever has a direct and immediate tendency to injure the school in its important interests, or to subvert the authority of those in charge of it, is properly a subject for regulation and discipline, and this is so wherever the acts may be committed.

Burdich v. Babcock, 31 *Iowa,* 562.

There is a limit to the powers of the school directors, and that limit is the needfulness or reasonableness of the rule. Thus, where a rule forbade the attendance of pupils upon social parties, and where a pupil was expelled for a violation thereof, it was held that the board had power to make all needful rules for the government of pupils while at school, but no power to follow them home and govern their conduct while under the parental eye; and that in prescribing the rule it had gone beyond its power.

Dritt v. Snodgrass, 66 *Mo.,* 286.

But in the same state it was held that a rule forbidding pupils from fighting and using profane language on the way to and from school was good, and that punishment could be inflicted for a violation thereof.

Deskins v. Gose, 85 *Mo.,* 585.

Teachers should remember that the rule makers are the directors.

State v. Barton, 45 *Wis.,* 150.

Morrow v. Wood, 35 *Wis.,* 50.

Wherever, however, it is absolutely necessary for the teacher to act in order to preserve the school from anarchy, or to maintain order and discipline, he is justified in so doing without waiting for an order of the directors. Wherever the exercise of this right is not called for by present necessity, it should be deferred for action by the board.

State ex rel, etc. v. Barton, 45 *Wis.,* 150.

Neither the teacher with a legal certificate and lawfully employed, nor the board of school directors, are liable in damages for tort by reason of having expelled a child from school, so long as they act in good faith. If they err in good faith in the discharge of their duties they are not liable.

Donahue v. Richards, 38 *Me.,* 376.

Sewell v. Board of Education, 29 *Ohio St.,* 89.

Spear v. Cummings, 23 *Pich.,* 22.

Boyd v. Blaisdel, 15 *Ind.,* 73.

Stephenson v. Hall, 14 *Barb.,* 222.

But where the child is entitled to go to school and the expulsion is wrongful, see *contra.*

Roe v. Deming, 21 *Ohio St.,* 666.

To make either liable there must be malice.

Dritt v. Snodgrass, 66 *Mo.,* 286.

Commonwealth v. Seed, 5 *Pa., L. J. R.,* 78.

Nor is the teacher liable on an implied contract to teach. There is no implied contract in the public schools between teacher and pupil. The only contract is with the board of directors to whom he is accountable for his acts, unless he is stirred by malicious motives and renders himself amenable to law.

SCHOOL LAWS.

Steckey v. Churchman, 2 *Bradw.* (*Ill.*), 584.

In Michigan it has been held that before expulsion or suspension may be adjudged against pupils who in any way deface or injure the school building, outhouses, furniture, maps or anything else belonging to the school, that such injury or defacement must be shown to be wilful and malicious. A careless act will not sustain the rule, even though the pupil be too poor to make satisfaction.

Holman v. School Trustees of Avon, Supreme Court Reports, 1889.

Directors, in the absence of promulgated rules, may suspend or expel, whenever upon due examination they become satisfied that the interests of the school demand such expulsion, any pupil who transgresses unwritten but well-defined rules of conduct prescribed by common sense and decency.

State v. Hamilton, 42 *Mo. App.*, 24.

See also,

Holman v. Trustees, 77 *Mich.*, 605.

AS TO RULES GENERALLY.

Sections 7041, 7042 and 7060 place the rule-making power with the directors. The power ordinarily given and its extent has been well expressed by the learned judge in *Rulison v. Post*, 79 *Ill.*, 567. He said:

" In the performance of their duty in carrying the law into effect, the directors may prescribe certain rules and regulations for the government of the schools in their district, and enforce them. They may, no doubt, classify the scholars, regulate their studies and their deportment, the hours to be taught, besides the performance of other duties necessary to promote the success and secure the well-being of such schools. But all such rules and regulations must be reasonable, and calculated to promote the objects of the law—the conferring of such an education upon all, free of charge. The law having conferred upon each child of proper age the right to be taught the enumerated branches, any rule or regulation which by its enforcement would tend to hinder or deprive the child of this right can not be sustained. All rules must be adapted to the promotion and accomplishment of this great and paramount object of the law."

Now, what are reasonable rules?

In *Thompson v. Beaver*, 63 *Ill.*, 353, the following conclusion was reached:

"What are reasonable rules is a question of law, and we do not hesitate to declare that a rule that would bar the doors of the school house against little children who had come from so great a distance (one and one-half miles) in the cold winter, for no other reason than that they were a few minutes tardy, is unreasonable and therefore unlawful. In its practical operation it amounts to little less than wanton cruelty."

Among the rules established by the board in a certain district was this:

"All pupils will be required to bring written excuses from their parents to teachers for absence, and such excuses must be satisfactory and reasonable, otherwise they will not be granted."

The court commented upon the rule as follows:

"The rule in question is not a hard or harsh one. It does not of itself indicate any sinister or malevolent purpose, or wicked force, on the part of the directors. It does not trench upon .the rights or dignity of any one. We instantly and properly repel any encroachment upon our rights as citizens. We have a proper pride and ambition in maintaining these rights under any and all circumstances. But I am utterly unable to understand how this simple rule or regulation, requiring the pupil in certain cases to bring a written excuse from its parents to the teacher, is an attack upon, or an abridgment of, our inalienable rights as citizens of this free country."

Churchill v. Fewkes, 13 *Ill. App.* (13 *Brad.*), 520.

The directors may make and enforce a rule forbidding the use of tobacco or whisky in any form, or the carrying of any deadly weapon, in any school room or in any part of the school building.

ENFORCEMENT OF RULES BY CORPORAL PUNISHMENT.

The following summary of cases will give an idea of what has been held with reference to corporal punishment in schools by courts of last resort in other states.

"The right of the parent to keep the child in order and obedience is secured by the common law. He may lawfully correct his child, being under age, in a reasonable manner, for this is for the benefit of his education. He may delegate, also, a part of his parental authority, during his life, to the tutor or schoolmaster of his child, who is then in *loco parentis*, and has such portion of the power of the parent committed to his charge—viz.: that of restraint and correction—as may be necessary to answer the purpose for which he is employed.

1 *Black., Com.*, 453, 454.
1 *Hale's P. C.*, 473, 474.

"The rights of parents (over their children) result from their duties. As they are bound to maintain and educate their children, the law has given them the right to such authority; and, in support of that authority, a right to the exercise of such discipline as may be requisite for, the discharge of their sacred trust. 'The power allowed by law to the parent over the person of the child may be delegated to a tutor or instructor, the better to accomplish the purposes of education.'"

Kent's Com., 169, 170.

Although the town school is instituted by the authority of the statute, the children are to be considered as put in charge of the instructor for the same purpose, and be clothed with the same power as when he is directly employed by the parents. The power of the parent to restrain and coerce obedience in children can not be doubted, and it has seldom or never been denied. The power delegated to the master by the parent must be accompanied for the time being with the same right, as incidental, or the object sought must fail of accomplishment.

"The practice, which has generally prevailed in our town schools since the settlement of the country, has been in accordance with the law thus expressed, and resort has been had to personal chastisement when a milder means of restraint had been unavailing."

Stevens v. Fassett, 27 *Me.*, 266.

" The law having elevated the teacher to the place of the parent, if he is still to sustain that sacred relation, it become him to be careful in the exercise of his authority, and not make his power a pretext for cruelty and oppression."

14 *Johns. R.*, 119.

" Whenever he undertakes to exercise it, the cause must be sufficient, the instrument suitable to the purpose; the manner and extent of the correction, the part of the person to which it is applied, the temper in which it is afflicted; all should be distinguished with the kindness, prudence and propriety which becomes the station."

Cooper v. McJunkin, 4 *Ind.*, 291.

The law, as we deem it to exist, is this: A schoolmaster has the right to inflict reasonable corporal punishment. He must exercise reasonable judgment and discretion in determining when to punish, and to what extent. In determining upon what is a reasonable punishment various considerations must be regarded—the nature of the offense, the apparent motive and disposition of the offender, the influence of his example and conduct upon others, and the sex, age, size and strength of the pupil to be punished. Among reasonable persons much difference prevails as to the circumstances which will justify the infliction of punishment, and the extent to which it may properly be administered. On account of this difference of opinion, and the difficulty which exists in determining what is a reasonable punishment, and the advantage which the master has by being on the spot to know all the circumstances—the manner, looks, tone, gestures and language of the offender (which are not always easily described), and thus to form a correct opinion as to the necessity and extent of the punishment, considerable allowance should be made to the teacher by way of protecting him in the exercise of his discretion. Especially should he have this indulgence when he appears to have acted from good motives and not from anger or malice. Hence, the teacher is not to be held liable on the ground of excess of punishment unless the punishment is clearly excessive, and would be so held in the general judgment of reasonable men. If the punishment be thus clearly excessive, then the master should be held liable for such excess, though he acted from good motives in inflicting the punishment, and in his own judgment considered it necessary and not excessive. But if there is any reasonable doubt whether the punishment was excessive, the master should have the benefit of the doubt."

Lander v. Slaver, 32 *Vt.*, 114.

In *State v. Mizner*, 59 *Ia.*, the supreme court approved the following instructions:

" In the absence of all proof, the law presumes that a father or school teacher punishes a child of the father or the pupil of the teacher for a reasouable cause and in a moderate and reasonable manner. But this presumption, like all other legal presumptions, may be rebutted by the proof.

"The legal objects and purposes of punishment in schools are like the objects and purposes of the state in punishing the citizens. They are threefold. First, the reformation and the highest good of the pupil; second, the enforcement and maintenance of correct discipline in school; and third, as an example to like evil-doers. And in no case can the punishment be justifiable unless it is inflicted for some definite offense or offenses which the pupil has committed, and the pupil is given to understand what he or she is being punished for. And if you find from the evidence that the punishment in this case was inflicted upon the prosecutrix without her knowing what she was being punished for, then the punishment was wrong on the part of the defendant. Punishment inflicted when the reason of it is unknown to the punished, is subversive and not promotive of the true objects of punishment, and can not be justified."

It was also held that any punishment with a rod which left marks or welts on the person of the pupil for two months afterward, or much less time, was immoderate and excessive, and that the court would have been jusrified in so instructing the jury. In this case the pupil was punished by the teacher because, acting under the direction of her father, she did not study algebra or attend school at the hours fixed. The court held that such a violation of rules should be punished by suspension or expulsion and not by whipping.

"We hold, therefore, that it may be laid down as a general rule, that teachers exceed the limits of their authority when they cause lasting mischief; but act within the limits of it when they inflict temporary pain.

"Within the sphere of this authority the master is the judge when correction is required, and of the degree of correction necefsary; and, like all others intrusted with a discretion, he can not be made personally responsible for error of judgment, but only for wickedness of purpose.

"But the master may be punishable when he does not transcend the powers granted, if he grossly abuse them. If he use his authority as a cover for malice, and under pretense of administering correction gratify his own bad passions, the mask of the judge shall be taken off, and he will stand amenable to justice as an individual not invested with judicial power."

State v. Pendergrass, 2 *Dev. & Bat.*, 365.

"If, inflicting punishment upon his pupil, he went beyond the limit of moderate castigation, and, either in the mode or degree of correction, was guilty of any unreasonable and disproportionate violence or force he was clearly liable for such excess in a criminal prosecution."

1 *Hawk.*, *c*. 60, *sec*. 23.
Kussell on Crimes, 7*th Amer. Ed.*, 755.
Bac. Ab. Assault and Battery, *C. J.*

"It is undoubtedly true, that, in order to support an indictment for an assault and battery, it is necessary to show that it was committed *ex intentione*, and that if the criminal intent is wanting the offense is not made out. But this intent is always inferred from the unlawful act. The unreasonable and excessive use of force on the person of another being proved, the wrongful intent is a necessary and legitimate conclusion in all cases where the act was designedly committed. It then becomes an assault and battery, because purposely inflicted without justification or excuse. Whether, under all the facts, the punishment of the pupil is excessive, must be left to the jury."

Commonwealth v. Randall, 4 *Gray*, 36.

"In inflicting such punishment the teacher must exercise sound discretion and judgment, and must adapt it not only to the offense but to the offender. Horace Mann, a high authority in the matter of schools, says of corporal punishment: 'It should be reserved for baser faults. It is a coarse remedy, and should be employed upon the coarse sins of our animal nature, and, when employed at all, should be administered in strong doses.' Of course the teacher, in inflicting such punishment, must not exceed the bounds of moderation. No precise rule can be laid down as to what shall be considered excessive or unreasonable punishment."

Reeve's Dom. Rel., 288.

"Each case must depend upon its own circumstances. And we think it equally clear that he should also take into consideration the mental and moral qualities of the pupil, and, as indicative of these, his general behavior in school and his attitude towards his teacher becomes proper subjects of consideration.

"We think, therefore, that the court acted properly in admitting evidence of the prior and habitual misconduct of the plaintiff, and that it was perfectly proper for the defendant, in chastising him, to consider not merely the immediate offense which had called for the punishment, but the past offenses that aggravated the present one, and showed the plaintiff to have been habitually refractory and disobedient. Nor was it necessary that the teacher should, at the time of inflicting the punishment, remind the pupil of his past and accumulating offenses. The pupil knew them well enough without having them freshly brought to his notice."

Shelton v. Sturgess, 53 *Conn.*, 481.

If a pupil who is of age attends school, she submits herself to all the rules of the school and to like discipline with those pupils who are under age.

State v. Mizner, 45 *Ia.*, 248.

The same rule holds if the pupil is over twenty-one years of age and attends the school by consent of the directors.

Stevens v. Fassett, 27 *Me.*, 266.

In *Peck v. Smith*, 41 *Conn.*, 442, the judge held that a member of a school board may eject a pupil from the school house for insulting conduct towards him:

"The defendant, being at the school house performing certain duties connected with the school, called the attention of the plaintiff to certain acts, not specially culpable in character, which he acknowledged he had committed. His bearing and manner were insolent and offensive, and the language in which he indulged was grossly profane. Such language, reprehensible at all times, should not have been allowed to pass with impunity from a school boy of the older class, within the walls of a school house, in the presence and hearing of younger pupils. After being told to leave he so conducted himself that it was proper to remove him, no unnecessary force being used to attain that object.

"It may be proper to observe, however, that public sentiment does not now tolerate such corporal punishment of pupils as was formerly thought permissible and even necessary."

1 *Cooley's Blackstone*, 453.

Rules which should control the teacher in inflicting punishment. The opinions of the highest judicial tribunals and eminent jurists concur in respect to the propriety and necessity of granting school teachers authority to inflict corporal punishment in certain cases, and of protection to them in the prudent and reasonable exercise of such authority either to promote the welfare of the child or the welfare of the whole school. Teachers are, however, held to a just accountability for the abuse of the power conferred. The decisions cited relate to punishments with the rod, ferule, etc., but the rule of discretion and accountability is the same for all other forms of punishment. Without doubt the best teachers do, as a general rule, use the rod least, because they have a more perfect personal discipline, and command a wider range of mental and moral resources from which to draw in dealing with the wayward and erring; and because they have, by nature, the faculty of dealing easily and successfully with youth. It may be that if we all were wise enough, some other remedy might be found in every case; I cannot say. But it is quite certain that, so far as we can judge of cause and effect, cases arise at one time or another in the experience of most teachers, when the timely and judicious infliction of corporal punishment seems, both at the time and afterwards, the wisest and best thing that could be done. Certain it is, also that castigation with the rod is often less cruel than sharp words, tones of irony, sarcasm or invective, and less humiliating and harmful than some of the substitutes therefor.

Illinois School Laws and Decisions.

SEC. 7061. They may permit older persons to attend the school under such regulations as they may deem proper. *Ib., part sec. 76.*

SEC. 7062. The county court shall have power, upon the petition of any person residing in any particular school district, to transfer the children or wards of such person, for educational purposes, to an adjoining district in the same county, or to an adjoining district in an adjoining county; *Provided*, Said petitioner shall state under oath that the transfer is for school purposes alone. *Provided, further,*

Where a number of colored children or wards, not exceeding ten, reside in a particular school district, the county court shall have power, upon the petition of any person, to transfer said colored children or wards of such person to an adjoining district in the same county, or an adjoining district in an adjoining county; and, also, where a number of white children or wards, not exceeding ten, reside in a particular school district, the county court shall have power, upon the petition of any person, to transfer said white children or wards of such person to an adjoining district in the same county, or an adjoining district in an adjoining county; and said transfers under the last named proviso shall not destroy the legality of such school districts, although the number of children be reduced to a number less than thirty-five persons of scholastic age; and said petitioner shall at once notify the county examiner of the county or counties and the directors of both districts. *Act April 3, 1891.* See *sec. 6988.*

It must be remembered that the right is a personal one and reaches no further than the children or wards of the person asking it. It does not transfer the tenants of the person nor any one living upon his estate. Tenants are not serfs and may not be transferred *nolens volens* upon the petition of the landlord.

The transfer can only be made to adjoining districts. The practice of transferring to distant districts not adjoining is pernicious and unlawful.

SEC. 7063. The directors of the district to which such children have been transferred, at the time of the enumeration shall include such children in the district to which they have been transferred, and they shall not be enumerated in the district where they reside. The district school tax of such person shall be added to the school revenues of the pistrict to which he has been transferred, and shall not be included in the school revenues of the district where he resides.

A transfer into a new district places the children and all the taxes for school purposes of thn party transferred in the district to which said party transfers. The party thus transferred can vote and hold office in said district, provided said party is not transferred out of his own township. See following section.

SEC. 7064. Any person who transfers his child, children or wards and property to any district for educational purposes, shall have the same right to vote in said district for directors and tax as other electors have of the district to which he is so transferred. Where such person is transferred to a district out of his county, the county treasurer of the county wherein he resides, shall open an account with the district to which he is transferred, and his school taxes shall be credited to the same and paid on the warrants of the directors of the district to which he is transferred. *Provided*, Any person transferring his property and children to an adjoining school district, for educational purposes, shall not have the right to vote for directors or tax out of his county, and to vote only in the political township in which he resides. *Dec. 7, 1875, sec. 76, as amended by act March 30, 1883, sec. 1.*

SEC. 7065. The directors may permit a private school to be taught in the district school house during such time as the said house is not occupied by a public school, unless they be otherwise directed by a majority of the legal voters of the district. *Act December 7, 1875, sec. 77.*

SEC. 7066. The directors shall cause the public schools in their districts to be closed on the days appointed for public examination of teachers in their county, and also cause the said school to be closed during the session of the teachers institute; *Provided*, Said schools shall not be closed for a greater length of time than five days during any one session of not more than five months. *Act March 27, 1885.*

By Act XXVII, approved March 5, 1895, so much of this section as relates to public examinations is repealed. Teachers are not now required to attend examinations unless they desire to obtain license to teach. No examination and institute can be held at the same time. Teachers are required to attend an institute of one week each year and cannot be charged for loss of time while attending. See sec. 7073.

SEC. 7067. Directors and county examiners shall be exempt from working on roads and highways. *Act December 7, 1875, secs. 77-79, as amended by act March 23, 1891.*

SEC. 7068. Any director or other person whose duty it may become to report to the county court the per cent. of tax levied by any school district at an annual meeting, and who shall neglect or refuse to do so in the manner and at the time provided by law, shall be liable for all loss which may be sustained by such failure and for all costs, and shall be fined not less than ten nor more than fifty dollars.

SEC. 7069. Within fifteen days after any special tax shall be voted by a school district at an annual meeting, it shall be the duty of the directors to furnish the county clerk with a certified list of all persons owning property in the district liable to pay such special tax.

SEC. 7070. Any person whose duty it is to execute sections 7046, 7069 or 7084, and who shall fail to do so, shall be fined not less than ten nor more than fifty dollars, and the same shall be paid into the county treasury. *Act March 11, 1881, secs. 1, 3 and 9.*

TEACHERS.

SEC. 7071. Any person who shall teach in a common school in this state, without a certificate of his qualification and his license to teach, shall not be entitled to receive for such services any compensation from revenues raised by tax or in any wise appropriated for the support of common schools; *Provided,* If his license expire by limitation during any school, such expiration shall not have the effect to interrupt his school, or to debar his claim against school revenues for the payment of teacher's wages.

The right to teach is based upon an approved examination before a state officer. Every teacher must show a certificate or not receive state revenue. This includes all assistants. The assistant is a teacher and can only receive compensation lawfully through the directors. No principal can draw a lump salary from the school revenues to pay for either licensed or unlicensed assistants. Each teacher must have a separate contract and draw his separate compensation.

The treasurer is warranted in demanding the license and the contract before paying any warrant; and if such contract discloses the fact that the warrant is drawn to cover the salary of an unlicensed teacher, it should not be paid. See secs. 7052, 7051 and 7043.

The teacher must have a living license on the day he begins the actual work of teaching. Having begun his school lawfully he may finish it, although his license expires before the end of his term. This, however, does not preclude the board of directors from demanding of each applicant a license which shall cover the entire term provided for in the contract.

The district is entitled to the services of a teacher qualified under the law and no act of the directors can bind the district to pay for the services of an incompetent man.

Deval v. School District No. 3, Michigan Supreme Court Reports, 1889.

As elsewhere stated, all funds collected from taxes levied by school directors, must be held subject to and paid out upon the orders of the directors of the district. But the orders on such tax funds must be for the payment of debts legally contracted and no others. Hence a board of directors cannot use any portion of such special district taxes to pay a teacher who taught without having the necessary certificate of qualifications. Directors are empowered to levy taxes for the sole purpose of supporting or extending the terms of such schools, and such only as the law contemplates. But the law does not contemplate or in any manner recognize, schools taught by teachers who have no certificates, and no public or special tax fund can, therefore, be used to pay any of the expenses of schools so taught. Any other interpretation of the statute would be absurd, because if the directors may ignore every other provision in respect to certificates, they may ignore every other provision of the act, and levy taxes to pay the teachers of writing schools, singing schools, or any other description of schools, however unlike they may be to the public schools provided for in the statute.

Casey v. Baldridge, 15 *Ill.,* 65.

Wells v. People, 71 *Ill.,* 532.

Directors who pay a teacher who has not a certificate are personally liable for the loss of school funds through their misuse of them. The school taught by a teacher without a certificate is not a legal school; and if, on that account, the district loses its share of funds distributed by the trustees, the directors are further liable personally for such loss. They are also liable to a fine for a failure to perform their duty under the law.

If directors employ a teacher who has not a certificate, as required by law, and the treasurer knows the fact, even if the directors certify to his schedule, the treasurer can not pay it. It would be a case of open violation of a positive requirement of the law, and should not be overlooked. Known and palpable fraud always vitiates.

Any interested tax-payer may enjoin the payment of a teacher who has no certificate, or may stop the payment of a judgment in favor of such teacher, if obtained by collusion with the directors.

Barr v. Deniston, 19 *N. H.*, 170.
Noble v. Directors, 117 *Ill.*, 30.

If a teacher teaches for a while without a certificate and then gets one, the directors can not pay for the time taught without a certificate. Neither can they pay him indirectly for such time by hiring him over at an advance in salary sufficient to make up for the time taught before he got a certificate. Public officers must not do indirectly what the law forbids them to do directly.

Wells v. People, 71 *Ill.*, 532.

Substitutes and assistants must have certiocates. The teacher employed as a substitute for however short a time, must have a certificate of qualification, make a schedule, and comply with all other requirements of the law, or the public funds can not be used in payment of temporary services so rendered. One teacher can not receive wages on the certificate of another, or in the name of another teacher.

All assistant teachers, special teachers of writing, etc., included, in the public schools, must have certificates of qualification from the county examiner—there is no exception to the emphatic requirements of the law in respect to certificates.

This opinion is grounded upon the plain object of the legislature in requiring teachers to possess certificates; which can be none other than to secure the employment of teachers of approved character and ability—a consideration of quite as much moment in the case of assistant teachers, as any other.

It is held that the superintendent of city and village schools belongs to the teaching force, and should, therefore, have a certificate of qualification in order that he may draw his pay.

When the directors persist, in violation of law, in retaining a teacher who does not hold a certificate, any tax-payer or patron of the school would be entitled to an injunction to restrain the teacher or board from continuing the school. The county superintendent can not take out an injunction in such a case.

Perkins v. Wolf, 17 *Ia.*, 228.
Barr v. Deniston, 19 *N. H.*, 170.

SEC. 7072. Every teacher shall keep a daily register of his school in the manner prescribed by law, and indicated by the blank school register to be furnished by the directors at the commencement of his school.

Directors cannot make the reports required by law without the information contained in this register, and they should exact rigidly a compliance with the requirements of this section. No teacher who refuses to comply with law or who is unable to comply therewith should be retained as a teacher, and the proper steps should be taken at once to revoke his license.

Directors must not draw warrant for last month's salary until this register is completed for the term.

ACT XXVII.

Sec. 7073. An act to amend section 7073 of Sandels & Hill's Digest.

SECTION
1. Only teachers to be examined for position in public schools of any county required to attend examinations in county.
2. Teachers in public schools shall attend county normal once a year.
3. Normal institute and quarterly examination shall not be held at same time.
4. No teacher attending either shall be charged with loss of time.

Be it enacted by the General Assembly of the State of Arkansas:

That section seven thousand and seventy-three of Sandels & Hill's Digest be amended so as to read as follows :

Section 1. It shall be the duty of only such teachers as desire to be examined for license to teach in the public schools of any county to attend any public examination for teachers in said county.

Sec. 2. It shall be the duty of all the teachers of the public schools to attend one institute annually, which shall be held by the county examiner, after having given twenty days' notice of the time and place of the institute in the same manner as is now required by law for quarterly examinations.

Sec. 3. No institute and quarterly examination shall be held at the same time.

Sec. 4. No teacher, when attending a quarterly examination, or an institute, shall be charged for loss of time while necessarily absent from his school to attend such examination or institute.

Approved March 5, 1895.

There is no way to avoid this duty, nor is it lawful for directors to encourage teachers in a wilful violation of law. It is still worse when they try to force teachers to do this by reservations in the contract. No teacher is bound by any contract which requires him to violate the law.

Teachers must attend these institutes. This law only excuses them from the examinations while they hold certificates.

SEC. 7074. No teacher employed in any of the common schools shall permit sectarian books to be used as a reading or text-book in the school under his care.

The law leaves the discretion of reading or not reading the Bible with the school boards, and the courts have uniformly refused to restrain, coerce or interfere with this discretion.

Board of Education of Cincinnati v. Minor, 23 *Ohio Stat.*, 211.
McCormich v. Burt., Northwestern Reporter, Illinois Supplement, Vol 1, *p*. 340.

The use of any version of the Bible as a text-book in the public schools, and the stated reading thereof in such schools by the teachers, without restriction, although unaccompanied by any comment, was held by the supreme court of Wisconsin in *State v. Board of Education* (76 *Wis.*, 177), as having a tendency to inculcate sectarian ideas, and such use enjoined.

It was held however that text-books founded upon the fundamental teachings of the Bible, or which contain extracts therefrom, and such portions of the Bible as are not sectarian, might be used in the secular instruction of the pupils and to inculcate good morals.

This is the latest legal deliverances upon this important subject and deserves the most careful study of all educators.

SEC. 7075. Any teacher who shall have complied with the provisions of this act shall be paid from the first money received into the county treasury to the credit of the district; and his claim shall not be superseded by any subsequent claim (*u*); and no money in the county treasury belonging to any district shall, so long as there is any such claim filed against the said district, be applied to any purposes whatever other than the payment of teachers' wages. *Act December 7, 1875, secs. 80-84.*

SEC. 7076. No teacher shall be entitled to the last month's pay for any school taught by him until he shall have returned to the directors of the district in which such school was taught the daily register furnished him, with all statistical work which teachers are by law required to perform, perfected and complete, and no director shall otherwise issue an order for such last month's pay. *Act March 11, 1881, sec. 4.*

(*u*.) See *sec.* 7081.

TRESPASS ON SCHOOL HOUSES, ETC.

Sec. 7077. Any person who shall wilfully destroy or injure any building used as a school house, or for other educational purposes, or any furniture, fixtures or apparatus thereto belonging, or who shall deface, mar or disfigure any such building, furniture or fixtures, by writing, cutting, painting or pasting thereon any likeness, figure, words or device, without the consent of the teacher or other person having control of such house, furniture, or fixtures shall be fined in a sum double the value of any such building, furniture, fixtures or apparatus so destroyed, and shall be fined in a sum not less than ten nor more than fifty dollars for each offense for writing, painting, cutting or pasting in any such building, furniture or fixtures any such words, figures, likeness or device, to be recovered by civil action in any court of competent jurisdiction; and the punishment provided in this section is in addition to, and not in lieu of, the punishment provided by the statutes for such offenses (v). *Act December 7, 1875, sec. 86.*

SCHOOL WARRANTS (w)—DISBURSEMENTS OF FUNDS, ETC.

Sec. 7078. It shall be unlawful for county collectors and treasurers to purchase or otherwise be the owners of or interested, directly or indirectly, in any school warrant issued by any school director of the county in which they reside.

Sec. 7079. The district school tax in each county may be payable and receivable in the warrants drawn by the directors of the school district in which a school tax may be levied by the county court.

Sec. 7080. It shall be the duty of the county treasurer

(v.) For an offense committed by insulting a teacher in the presence of his pupils, see *sec.* 1539. For cutting, writing upon or defacing school-houses, see *sec.* 1794. For disturbing schools, see *sec.* 1798.

(w.) The statute of limitations runs on school warrants. *School District v. Croomer,* 52-454; *School District v. Reeve,* 56-68.

of each county to keep in his office a suitable and well-bound book, in which he shall register by number and in the order of presentation all district school warrants that may be presented to him; this registration to be made before the warrant is paid, and it shall show the date of the presentation of the warrant, by whom drawn, on what district and in whose favor, and for what purpose drawn, the amount and date of the warrant, date of payment, and to whom paid; and said book shall at all times be subject to the inspection of any tax-payer (x).

SEC. 7081. It shall be the duty of the county treasurers, immediately upon the receipt by them of any school funds, to give notice of the amount and kind of funds received, and from what source received, by written or printed notices put up in two public places in each and every school district and at the court-house door, and the funds so received shall be paid out *pro rata* on the warrants registered in accordance with the provisions of the preceding section (y); *Provided*, Application for such payment is made within thirty days from the giving of the notice herein required.

SEC. 7082. Any officer failing to comply with the requirements of this act for each and every offense, shall be subject to indictment, and, if found guilty, shall be punished by a fine of not less than five hundred dollars and by confinement in the penitentiary of the state for a period not less than three nor more than twelve months.

SEC. 7083. Any director who shall fraudulently issue any school warrant shall be guilty of a misdemeanor, and, upon conviction, shall be subject to the penalties enumerated in the preceding section. *Act May 27, 1874.*

SEC. 7084. The county treasurer shall, on or before the first day of September each year, forward to the superin-

---

(x.) The legislature may relieve the treasurer and his bondsmen from liability for school funds. *Pearson v. State*, 56-148.

(y.) See sec. 6993.

tendent of public instruction a certified statement showing the amount, in kind, of public school funds received by him; from what sources they were received; how and for what purposes they have been disbursed, and what amount, in kind, remains in the treasury. *Act March 11, 1881, sec. 8.*

SEC. 7085. The order of any board of directors, properly drawn after the passage of this act, other than those of single school districts in cities and towns, shall be presented to the treasurer of the proper county within sixty days after it was drawn by the said board of directors. All such orders shall be paid in the order of their presentation (*z*). *Act March 21, 1885, sec. 1.*

SEC. 7086. If there are no funds with which to pay such order, the treasurer shall indorse the same: "Not paid for want of funds," giving the date and signing his name officially. He shall number and record each warrant in the book provided for such purpose, keeping a separate record for each district, and shall pay said warrants in the order of their number. *Act March 21, 1885, sec. 2.*

VIOLATION OF SCHOOL LAWS—DUTY OF PROSECUTING ATTORNEYS.

SEC. 7087. The prosecuting attorney of each judicial district shall, upon being satisfied that any violation of the school laws of this state has been committed by any officer or person, in any county of his district, which renders such officer or person so offending liable to any fine, pain, penalty or forfeiture for damage, without delay, institute in any court of competent jurisdiction such proceeings as are necessary to bring such offender to trial, and secure to the county school district, or person damaged by such violation, the benefits and reliefs to which each or any of them may be entitled; and for such services the prosecuting attorney shall be allowed the same compensation as he is allowed in

---

(*z*.) See *School District v. Reeve*, 56-68.

cases of misdemeanor, which shall be assessed against such offender as cost. *Act March 11, 1881, sec. 10.*

SPECIAL ACT FOR THE REGULATION OF PUBLIC SCHOOLS IN CITIES AND TOWNS.

SEC. 7088. Any incorporated city or town in this state, including the territory annexed thereto for school pnrposes, may be organized into and established as a single school district in the manner and with the powers hereinafter specified. *Act February 4, 1869, sec. 1.*

SEC. 7089. Upon the written petition of twenty voters of such city or town, praying that the sense of the legal voters of said city or town may be taken on the adoption of this act for the regulation and government of the public schools therein, it shall be the duty of the mayor of such city or town, within five days after the presentation of such petition, to designate and fix a day, not less than seven nor more than fifteen days distant, for holding an election in said city or town for that purpose and also for the election by ballot, at the same time, of a board of six school directors for said city or town.

SEC. 7090. The mayor shall cause notice of said election to be given by posting notices in at least five public places in said city or town, and by one insertion in such newspapers as may be published in said city or town. The electors at said election desiring to vote in favor of the adoption of this act shall have written or printed on their ballots, "For the school law," and those opposed thereto shall have written or printed on their ballots, "Against the school law;" and, if a majority of the ballots cast at said election shall be "For school law," then, and in that case only, shall such city or town be deemed and held to be a single school district under and in pursuance of this act, and the directors voted for and elected at said election shall qualify and enter upon the discharge of their duties as hereinafter provided. *Ib., part sec. 2.*

SEC. 7091. On the third Saturday in May, 1893, and annually thereafter, an election shall be held at the usual voting place in each ward of all incorporated towns and cities heretofore organized into single or special school districts, for the election of two directors, who shall serve for three years, and until their successors are elected and qualified. The ballot of the voter, in addition to the names of the persons voted for as directors, shall have written or printed on it the words "for tax" or "against tax," and the rate the voter desires levied; *Provided*, In incorporated towns and cities of the second class, the election may be held at one or more of the voting places therein, and not in each ward, if the board of directors shall so direct by notice posted in three public places in said city or town ten days before the election designating the place or places at which said election shall be held.

SEC. 7092. Said election shall be held by the judges appointed to hold the municipal elections in said city or town next preceding the said election, for the ward or wards in which said school election may be held. The judges at each voting place shall appoint two clerks, and each judge and clerk shall take the oath required by law, and shall receive for their services the sum of one dollar each, to be paid out of the school fund of the district on the order of the board of directors.

The four preceding sections are to determine whether the special act for the regulation of public schools in cities and towns shall be adopted. They are preliminary to organization. They require the following *modus operandi:*

1. A written petition of twenty voters asking that the sense of the legal voters be taken on the adoption of the act.

2. The mayor must fix within five days from the presentation of said petition a day for said election.

3. Said election shall be not less than seven nor more than fifteen days from the date of the proclamation.

4. Said election shall also determine by ballot a board of six directors.

5. The mayor must promulgate the election notices by posting and by print ing should there be a paper.
6. The electors must vote by ballot and as prescribed.
7. A majority of all the votes cast are necessary to make said city or town a single school district.
8. A majority of all the votes cast is also necessary to elect each of the six directors. It results that the special act may be legally adopted and all or some part of the directory fail of an election. This failure will not affect the adoption of the special act, but said city or town will be a single school district with a vacancy or vacancies in the directory.

The following act provides how all vacancies on boards in special school districts are filled:

ACT LVI.

AN ACT to give notice of election in special school dis-districts and fill vacancy in school board.

SECTION
1. Notice of annual election to be given fifteen days prior to election. How.
2. Provides for filling vacancy on board.
3. Repeals all laws in conflict. Act takes effect from passage.

Be it enacted by the General Assembly of the State of Arkansas:

SECTION 1. When any special school district has been organized as provided by law, the board of directors shall give notice of each annual election at least fifteen days previous to such election, by posting notices in at least five public places in said district.

SEC. 2. That if the office of director in any special school district shall become vacant, the remaining directors of said district shall elect a director to fill such vacancy, who shall serve until the next annual election for school directors, at which time all vacancies shall be filled by the electors for the unexpired term.

SEC. 3. That all laws and parts of laws in conflict with this act be and are hereby repealed, and that this act take effect and be in force from and after its passage.

Approved March 26, 1895.

SEC. 7093. The judges shall cause the polls to be opened at nine o'clock and closed at sunset.

SEC. 7094. If any of the regular judges shall fail to appear by ten o'clock, the assembled voters, not less than ten in number, shall select other judges in their places.

SEC. 7095. If the election shall be held in all the wards of the city or town, each voter shall vote in the ward where he resides; *Provided*, Voters residing in any part of the district not embraced in any ward may vote at any place he may deem most convenient.

SEC. 7096. The returns of said election shall be made to the county clerk, who shall forthwith deliver a certificate of election to each of the persons elected directors.

SEC. 7097. He shall also declare the result of the votes for and against tax, and certify the same to the county court on the first day of the term fixed by law for levying county taxes; and the rate of taxes so certified shall be levied by the court as other school taxes.

SEC. 7098. Each person elected director shall take the oath of office within five days after receiving a certificate of election, which shall be filed with the county clerk, and thereafter during his term of office no further oath nor affidavit shall be required of him in the discharge of his official duties.

SEC. 7099. The provisions of chapter lvii shall have no application to the elections herein provided for. *Act April 10, 1893, secs. 1 7.*

SEC. 7100. Said board of directors shall organize by choosing from their own number a president and secretary, who shall hold their offices until the last Saturday in May, and annually, on that day, said board shall meet and elect from their number a president and secretary. *Act March 21, 1885, sec. 2.*

SEC. 7101. Said board of directors shall hold a regular meeting on the last Saturday in each month, and may hold stated meetings at such other times and places in said district as they may appoint; four members of said board shall constitute a quorum, but a less number may adjourn from time to time; special meetings thereof may be called by the president, or by any two members of the board, on giving one day's notice of the time and place of the same, and, in case of the absence of the president, a president *pro tempore* shall be chosen. The office of any member of said board, as such, who shall, without good cause, fail to attend three consecutive monthly or stated meetings of said board, may be declared vacant by the board. The board may make rules and regulations for their own government and for the dispatch and regulation of the school business and affairs of the district, not inconsistent with law. *Act February 4, 1869, sec. 4.*

SEC. 7102. Said board of directors shall have power to purchase or lease school house sites, to build, hire or purchase school houses, and to keep in repair and furnish the same with the necessary seats, desks, furniture, fixtures and fuel, and to insure the same; to fence the school grounds, erect out-houses, provide wells, and make all other improvements on the school house grounds and school houses belonging to said district necessary and proper for the comfort, convenience and health of the scholars, and the preservation of said property; to hire teachers for all public schools of the district (*aa*), employ a superintendent of the schools (*bb*), who may also be principal of any graded or high school that said board may establish; to provide books and apparatus for the schools, and the necessary blank books and stationery for the board, and school registers and the blanks for the teachers; to establish and maintain a sufficient number of primary, graded or high schools to accommodate all

---

(*aa*.) See *School District v. Maury*, 53-471.

(*bb*.) The power to employ a superintendent is not limited to the term of office of the board. *Gates v. School District*, 53-468.

In a suit for salary after unlawful discharge, for liability of board and measure of damages, see *Gates v. School District*, 57-370.

the scholars in said district (*cc*); to determine the branches to be taught and the text-books to be used in the several schools of the district (*dd*); to admit pupils not belonging to the district on such terms as they may agree upon with the parents or guardians of said pupils, or the district from whence they came ; to appoint a board of three visitors and examiners for the schools of the district, which board shall examine persons applying to teach in any of the schools in said district; *Provided,* No teacher shall be employed who does not hold a certificate from the state superintendent or county examiner ; to examine, from time to time, the books and accounts of the county treasurer, so far as the same relate to the several school funds belonging to the district ; and when, in the opinion of a majority of the members of said board, the best interests of the district demand a sale or exchange of any real estate or school-house site belonging to the district, they may sell or exchange the same, the deed therefor to be executed by the president of the board upon a majority vote of the whole board of directors authorizing and directing such sale or exchange. *Ib., sec. 5.*

This section does not authorize the directors to substitute their examination for that of the examiner. The examiner's rights are superior to those of the directors. He should examine under his oath, and license or refuse to license as his judgment decides, and is not accountable to any board of directors. Nor should he hold his examination in connection with the examination of the board. His work should be entirely separate from their work. They have the right to examine, but not to interfere in any particular with the examiner's work. Any regulation of a board of directors which requires the examiner's certificate to be granted only after an examination of city teachers in the presence of examiners appointed by the board is absolutely nugatory so far as the county examiner is concerned. His examinations should be separate from and entirely free from supervision of city examiners.

EXACTION OF FEES.

Under the constitution of Georgia, providing that public schools shall be free

---

(*cc.*) But no tax for any purpose can now be levied by the county court without a vote of the electors of the district. *Article* 14, *section* 3, *Const.; Cole v. Blackwell,* 38–271.

(*dd.*) See *secs.* 6975, 7046.

to all children, a municipal public school established under a local act cannot exact incidental fees from resident scholars.

Irvin v. Gregory, 86 *Ga.*, 605.

The following opinion of the attorney general should be carefully considered :

" In answer to your inquiries, I have the honor to say that, in my opinion, section 7043 applies as well to special or single school districts as to ordinary common school districts.

" I am also of opinion that it applies to the superintendent of schools in such special districts, provided he is to act as a teacher; otherwise not.

" I am also of the opinion that said section is mandatory upon the directors ; but I do not believe, or mean to be understood as saying, that a verbal contract made with a qualified teacher would be void because not in writing."

The following decision of the supreme court interprets the law very clearly :

REMOVAL OF A TEACHER FOR INCOMPETENCY.

Under sections 7102 and 7103, which enjoin the board of school directors to hire suitable teachers; to enforce all necessary rules for the government of teachers and pupils; and to visit the schools and observe the discipline and progress of the pupils, the board has the power to remove a teacher for incompetency and for immorality; and the fact that the teacher has been duly licensed by the county examiner, and that the latter has failed to revoke the license as he is empowered to do by section 7013, is not conclusive on the board as to the competency or morality of the teacher.

See *Dist. of Fort Smith v. Mansy*, 53 *Ark.*, 471.

The fact that the board has tolerated the teacher's misconduct and inefficiency for a time does not operate as a waiver of its right to discharge him therefor, as the teacher's undertaking to perform his duty in a moral and skilful manner is assumed for the benefit of the school, its pupils, and patrons, and not for the benefit of the board.

School District of Fort Smith v. Mansy, 53 *Ark.*, 471.

The following decision is so sound that it is introduced here as a guide to directors of this state:

" Non-residents. In a local statute authorizing the establishment of public schools in a town, a provision that the local board may admit pupils not residents of the town on such terms as the board may prescribe, does not permit the board to prescribe terms which would cast upon the town or its inhabitants any part of the expense of educating non-resident pupils. Such pupils can not be received at a less rate per scholar than the inhabitants of the town pay by taxation for their children, nor can they be received at all to the exclusion of resident children who would otherwise attend."

Irvin v. Gregory, 86 *Ga.*, 605.

SEC. 7103. It shall be the duty of said board, as soon as the means for that purpose can be provided, to establish in said district an adequate number of primary schools, so located as best to accommodate the inhabitants thereof; and it shall be the further duty of said board to establish in said district a suitable number of other schools of a higher grade or grades, wherein instruction shall be given in such studies as may not be provided for in the primary schools; the number of schools, the grades thereof, and the branches to be taught in each and all of said schools to be determined by said board. It shall be the duty of said board to keep said schools in operation not less than three nor more than ten months in each year. The said board shall have power to make and enforce all necessary rules and regulations for the government of teachers and pupils in said schools. Said board shall also, separately or collectively, together with such persons as they may appoint or invite, visit the schools in the district at least twice in each year, and observe the discipline, mode of teaching, progress of the pupils, and see that the teachers keep a correct register of the pupils, embracing the periods of time during which they attend school, the branches taught, and such other matters as may be required by law or by the instructions of the state superintendent. *Ib., sec. 6.*

SEC. 7104. No draft or warrant shall be drawn on the county treasurer, except in pursuance of an order of said board; all drafts or warrants on the treasurer shall be signed by the president, or president *pro tempore*, and the secretary, and shall specify the fund on which they are drawn and the use for which the money is assigned. *Ib., sec. 8.*

SEC. 7105. The secretary shall record all the proceedings of the board in books kept for that purpose; shall make and preserve copies of all reports required by law to be made to the state superintendent of public instruction or county examiner; shall file all papers transmitted to him pertaining to the business of the district; shall make, or cause to be made, the annual enumeration of the youth of the district in the time and manner required by law of school directors, and shall perform such other duties as the board of directors may order and direct; and for his services may be allowed reasonable compensation, to be audited and allowed by a majority of said board. The other members of said board shall receive no compensation for their services. *Ib., sec. 9.*

SEC. 7106. The title of all real estate and other property belonging, for school purposes, to any city or town organized into a separate school district under this act, shall vest, and hereby is vested, in said city or town, as a school district, and shall be under the management and control of the board of school directors for said district as fully and completely as other school property belonging to said district. *Ib., sec. 10.*

SEC. 7107. All school districts formed under and governed by this act shall be known by the name of the city or town constituting the district, with the words "School District of" prefixed thereto (as, for example, "School District of Little Rock"); and by such name, may sue and be sued, contract and be contracted with, purchase, acquire, hold and sell property, receive gifts, grants and bequests, and generally shall possess and enjoy all the corporate powers usually possessed by bodies corporate of like character. The style of the board of directors for school districts under this act shall be "Board of School Directors." *Ib., sec. 11.*

SEC. 7108. The board of school directors of any district organized under this act shall pay and discharge all debts and liabilities lawfully incurred by the several school districts existing under previous law and embraced in the district organized under this act. *Ib., sec. 12.*

SEC. 7109. Any person elected a director under the provisions of this act who shall fail to take the oath of office and qualify as herein required, or who, after qualifying as such director, shall fail to perform and discharge the official duties incumbent upon him as a director, shall be liable to the same penalties that now are or may be hereafter provided by law against directors of school districts for failing or refusing to qualify, or for neglect of official duty. *Ib., sec. 13.*

SEC. 7110. The board of directors may fix the term of office and define the duties of the board of visitors and examiners of the public schools in their district, and any person appointed by the board of directors a member of said board of visitors and examiners who shall refuse to act as such, and discharge the duties pertaining to such position, shall forfeit and pay to said district the sum of twenty-five dollars, to be recovered in civil action in the name of said district, and added to the teachers' fund belonging to said district. *Provided*, No person shall be compelled to serve in that capacity more than three consecutive years. Said board of visitors and examiners shall receive no compensation for their services. *Ib., sec. 14.*

SEC. 7111. All school districts organized under this act shall have and receive their full proportion and distributive share of the general school fund of the state, in the same manner and according to the same rule as it is or may be apportioned to other districts. *Ib., sec. 15.*

SEC. 7112. It shall be the duty of the state superintendent and county examiners to make such suggestions and recommendations to the board of directors in relation to organizing and conducting the public schools in the districts organized under this act as they shall deem important.

SEC. 7113. The provisions of the general school laws of the state which are now or may hereafter be in force, when not inapplicable, and so far as the same are not inconsistent with and repugnant to the provisions of this act, shall apply to districts organized under this act; and such provisions of said laws as are inconsistent with and repugnant to the provisions of this act and inapplicable to districts organized thereunder, shall have no operation, force or effect in such districts. The county court shall annex contiguous territory to single school districts under the provisions of this act, when a majority of the legal voters of said territory and the board of directors of said single district shall ask, by petition, that the same shall be done. *Ib., secs. 16 and 17.*

II—SCHOOL LANDS (*ee*).

SEC. 7114. Whenever the inhabitants of any congressional township in this state shall desire the sale of the sixteenth section of such township, or of any lands substituted therefor, or any which have been or may be mortgaged to the state of Arkansas for the use of the school fund, which after foreclosure and sale have been stricken off to the state of Arkansas; they may, by written petition, signed by a majority of the male inhabitants of such township, require the collector of taxes of the county wherein such land is situated to sell the same. *Act April 14, 1893.*

SEC. 7115. Upon the reception of such petition, the collector shall ascertain that it is signed by a majority of the male inhabitants of such township and shall immediately proceed to divide the land into forty-acre tracts, and after making such division, a statement or plat of the same and a number of each tract shall be made so that the boundaries may be defined and ascertained, which statement or plat of the sections shall be used as a guide in advertising and selling said lands. *Provided,* The collector may, when necessity requires it, call the county surveyor of his county to assist in such survey and division, and he shall be allowed and paid

---

(*ee.*) Directors can confer no authority to cut timber on school lands, and one who does so by their authority, under an agreement with them to pay the value, commits a trespass for which he may be sued by the state. *Widner v. State,* 49-172. The legal title to school lands is in the state, and a school district can not maintain an action for such lands. *Ib.; School District v. Driver,* 50-346. See *State v. Morgan,* 52-150.

out of the funds arising from the sale of such school lands by said collector such compensation as he is allowed by law for similar services, and the receipts of such surveyor to said collector shall be a sufficient voucher for the money so paid.

SEC. 7116. In subdividing the sixteenth section lands for sale, no tract shall contain more than forty acres, and the division may be made into town or city lots with roads, streets or alleys between them.

SEC. 7117. The collector shall cause each tract or subdivision of such school land to be appraised at a fair value by three disinterested householders of the county, each of whom shall take an oath which shall be indorsed upon the appraisement that he does not desire or intend to buy said land or any part thereof, and that he will not directly or indirectly be or become interested in the purchase thereof at the sale to be made by the collector; such appraisement shall be returned to the collector.

SEC. 7118. The collector shall then give notice that he will sell the said school lands at the court-house door of the county on the first day of the next term of the county court upon the terms prescribed by law. Such notice shall be published in some newspaper published in the county where the land is situated at least four weeks before the day of sale. If there be no newspaper published in said county, then the collector shall post up written notices in at least six of the most public places of the county four weeks before the day of sale.

The collector shall also in either case put up a copy of the notice upon the school house situated on the land, if there be one thereon; if not, at the most public place on the land.

SEC. 7119. Upon the day of sale the collector shall offer the lands at public auction in separate subdivisions, beginning with number one and ending with the last mentioned division. Such sale shall be made between the hours of 12 m. and 3 p. m., but may be continued from day to day at the same place and between the same hours until all have been sold or offered. The sale shall be made for cash. If any bidder shall fail to perfect his bid by paying the cash, the collector shall immediately resell the land and the bidder shall be responsible for the difference between his bid and the price at which the land sold, which may be recovered from him by the collector, in action for the use of the township, and the collector shall, if necessary, at once institute suit against such bidder to recover the amount of difference between his bid and the price at which the land sold. No tract or such division shall be sold for less than three-fourths of its appraised value. *Provided*, No tract or subdivision of the sixteenth section lands shall be sold at a less price than one dollar and twenty-five cents per acre. If any tract offered is not sold it may be offered again upon like notice, upon the first day of the next, or any succeeding term of the county court, and so on until sold without a new petition.

SEC. 7120. The collector shall, without delay, report all sales to the county court, which may reject or confirm the same. If any sale be rejected, the county court may direct the collector to again advertise and offer the land, and may specify the minimum price at which the tract or tracts may be sold, not to be less than two-thirds of its appraised value. *Provided*, No tract or subdivision of the sixteenth section lands shall be sold at a less price than one dollar and twenty-five cents per acre. If the sale be confirmed by the county court the collector shall execute and deliver to the purchaser a certificate in the following form :

I, ... collector in and for the county of .... , state of Arkansas, certify that .... has purchased .... of section .... , in township .... , range .... , containing .... acres at $ .... dollars per acre, and has paid to me in full the sum of $............ .... dollars. The expense of the sale was:

    Cost of advertising, $......................
    Cost of order of confirmation, $............ ... .
    Cost of rejection of prior sale, $... ... .
    Surveyor's fee (if any), $......... ....
    Collector's commission, ... per cent., $...... ....

    Leaving a net balance of $............ .. .. in my hands due the sixteenth (16) section fund account of this county.

Now, therefore, upon the presentation of this certificate to the commissioner of state lands, the said .... his heirs or assigns, shall be entitled to a deed from said commissioner of state lands for the tract or land above described.

                  Collector of.............. .... county.

In all cases proper orders of confirmation or rejection shall be entered on record by the county court.

SEC. 7121. Out of the money received by the collector for the sale or sales of the sixteenth section lands, he shall pay the cost of advertising, cost of confirmation order, cost of rejection of sale (if any), surveyor's fees (if any), and he may retain for his services two per cent. of the gross amount received by him for the sale of such land; the residue of the money received for the sale of said land, after deducting the expenses as are above provided for, he shall at once transmit to the treasurer of state, who shall place the amount to the credit of the county's sixteenth section fund to which it rightfully belongs.

SEC. 7122. The county clerks of the several counties in this state shall examine carefully and closely the tax books of their respective counties and ascertain what person or persons are paying taxes on any part or parts or the whole of the sixteenth section lands, and it shall be the further duty of the county clerks after ascertaining from the tax books the names of any person or persons paying taxes on any of the sixteenth section lands, and the numbers of said lands, to examine the record of deeds and find by what authority and whether any title or titles vest in said person or persons in whose name or names said lands are assessed, and shall on or before the first Monday in September, eighteen hundred and eighty-five, make and forward to the commissioner of state lands a full and complete statement of the exact status and condition of all of the sixteenth section lands in their respective counties. The county clerks shall be allowed the sum of forty dollars each for their services in making this report, and it shall be paid to them by their respective counties.

SEC. 7123. The county clerks of the several counties in this state shall keep in a well-bound book, provided for that purpose, correct and accurate accounts with each and every township in their several counties, which may be entitled to any of the funds under this act, and shall immediately after each and every sale of any part of said sixteenth sections certify to the auditor of state the amount of moneys received by such collectors on account of such sales, and the auditor shall thereupon charge the same to such collector.

SEC. 7124. A neglect, failure or refusal by any county clerk to perform any and all duties enjoined upon him by the provisions of this act, shall be deemed a misdemeanor, and, upon conviction thereof, such clerk shall be fined in any sum not less than one hundred dollars, nor more than five hundred dollars, for each offense, and may be removed from office.

ACT LX.

AN ACT to amend section 7114 of Sandels & Hill's Digest of the Statutes of Arkansas and for other purposes.

SECTION
1. Sixteenth section or equivalent lands may be sold upon petition of majority of voters.
2. Sheriff vested with powers of collector for purposes of this act.
3. Repeals laws in conflict. Act takes effect from passage.

Be it enacted by the General Assembly of the State of Arkansas:

SECTION 1. Whenever the inhabitants of any congressional township in this state shall desire the sale of the sixteenth section of such township, or of any lands substituted therefor, or any which have been or may be mortgaged to the state of Arkansas for the use of the school fund, which after foreclosure and sale have been stricken off to the state of Arkansas, they may, by written petition signed by a majority of the adult male inhabitants of such township, require the collector of taxes, or if there be no collector, then the sheriff of the county wherein such land is situated, to sell the same.

SEC. 2. That for the purpose of making sales of any of the lands mentioned in the preceding section, the sheriff is hereby vested with all powers now conferred by law upon collectors.

SEC. 3. That all laws and parts of laws in conflict herewith are hereby repealed, and this act take effect and be in force from and after its passage.

Approved March 26, 1895.

HOUSE MEMORIAL NO. 1.

Resolved by the Senate and House of Representatives of the State of Arkansas:

That our senators in congress be instructed and our representatives requested to use all their influence with the congress of the United States so as to change and modify the compact entered into between the United States and the state of Arkansas with regard to the "sections of land numbered sixteen in every township," and when such section has been sold or otherwise disposed of, other lands equivalent thereto, and as contiguous as may be "and granted to the state for the use of the inhabitants of such township for the use of the schools," so that the said lands or any funds now on hand derived from the sale or lease of same may be apportioned by the state to common school purposes for the promotion of education in said state. And that the governor transmit to our senators and representatives, respectively, a a copy of this resolution.

Approved March 26, 1895.

COLLECTION OF CLAIMS DUE COMMON SCHOOL FUND.

SEC. 7125. The attorney general of the state of Arkansas is authorized and instructed to employ competent attorneys residing in the counties in which the lands are situated to collect all claims and notes due the school fund arising from the sale of the sixteenth section lands. Before taking charge of any such notes or claims, each of said attorneys shall be required to give bond for the faithful keeping, collecting and accounting for same, as provided for in this act, in double the sum of the amount supposed to come into his hands, and such security as shall be approved by the circuit judge of the judicial circuit in which said attorney resides, and such bond when approved shall be filed with the commissioner of state lands, and the commissioner of state lands shall, when such bond has been filed with him, turn over, or cause to be turned over to the said attorney all notes and claims due the school fund pertaining to the sixteenth section lands. Said attorneys may retain, as fees for collection, ten per cent. of the gross amount collected by them under the provisions of this act (*ff*). The remainder of said gross amount, after deducting their fees, as above provided for, shall be by said attorneys transmitted without delay to the treasurer of state, who shall place the same to the credit of the sixteenth section fund of the county to which it rightfully belongs, and said attorneys shall prepare and forward to the commissioner of state lands a statement for each and every collection made by them, setting forth the name of the maker of the note or claim, the date of same, the dates of all previous payments (if any) made on such note or claim.

(*ff*) See *Wallace v. State*, 54-611.

S—7

SEC. 7126. All moneys paid into the state treasury arising from the sale or the collection of notes and claims pertaining to the sixteenth section lands, shall be by the state treasurer placed to the credit of the county's sixteenth section fund, to which said moneys may rightfully belong, and the treasurer of state shall, for each payment to him on account of the sixteenth section fund, issue triplicate receipts, one of which receipts shall be filed with the auditor of state, one filed with the commissioner of state lands and one given to the party making payment.

SEC. 7127. The treasurer of state shall, by and under direction of the board of commissioners of the common school fund, as soon as practicable after the receipt of any moneys paid into the state treasury on account of the sixteenth section fund, invest the same in either United States bonds or bonds of the State of Arkansas, and as interest accrues on said investment he shall collect the same and place to the credit of the respective counties' sixteenth section fund accounts such interest on said investment, in the proportion to which each county is properly entitled.

SEC. 7128. The interest, accruing to the several counties and townships, that may hereafter be in the state treasury, shall be drawn out of the treasury in the same manner as now provided by law for drawing other funds due counties, and when drawn shall be accounted for by the county treasurer in the same manner as for other county funds thus drawn, and the county court shall distribute and set apart to the proper townships all such sums and funds as shall be due such township, either from the sales of sixteenth sections in such townships or from collections of notes belonging thereto.

SEC. 7129. All notes, claims, bonds, papers or evidences of debt belonging to the school fund, arising from the sale or sales of the sixteenth section lands, in the hands of county collectors or other persons, shall be, within ninety days after the passage of this act, turned over to the commissioner of state lands.

SEC. 7130. All county treasurers, collectors, or other persons, having in their possession any funds arising from the sale or sales of the sixteenth section lands, shall, within ninety days after the passage of this act, pay the same into the state treasury, and the state treasurer shall place the same to the credit of the respective counties' sixteenth section fund accounts to which said funds do rightfully belong.

SEC. 7131. That upon the presentation to the commissioner of state lands of any certificate of purchase as specified in section 7120 the commissioner shall execute to the purchaser a deed for the lands therein described, and shall keep a full and complete record of all such sales and of the deeds so issued, and it shall be the further duty of the commissioner of state lands to keep as correct records of sale or sales of the sixteenth section lands as the reports made to him from time to time may enable him to do. *Act March 31, 1885, secs. 2–18.*

PATENTS (*gg*).

SEC. 7132. When the purchaser of any portion of the common school lands has heretofore assigned, or may hereafter assign, the certificate of purchase of such land, the title thereof may be made directly to the last assignee of such certificate of purchase, upon full payment of all the purchase money and interest due on said land. *Act April 12, 1869, sec. 10.*

SEC. 7133. If any person who shall have purchased any portion of the sections of school lands from the collector of any of the counties of this state, and paid one-fourth the purchase money therefor, and received a bond for title from such collector, shall die before such payment is fully made, and the executor, administrator, guardian or legal represent-

---

(*gg*.) See *State v. Morgan*, 52–150.

ative of such deceased person shall pay or cause to be paid the balance, if any, that shall be due to the collector on said purchase, upon the certificate of the collector of the proper county that the whole of the purchase money, with all the interest due thereon, has been fully paid, the commissioner of state lands shall forthwith execute a deed, as is now required by law, to the heirs at law of such deceased person (*hh*). *Ib*., sec. *11, as amended act February 16, 1885*,

SEC. 7134. The land thus conveyed to the heirs shall stand charged with the amount of money necessarily advanced to the school fund, in order to procure title, and shall, in other respects, be chargeable with the rights and incumbrances that would have attached had it descended regularly to the same heirs. *Ib*.

SEC. 7135. All patents issued for sixteenth section, or any part thereof, or common school land during the war between the states and all the official acts of the officers of this state, in regard to such lands, during the said war, and also all deeds made by the common school commissioners of the several counties in compliance with an act of the legislature of the state, entitled, "An act to relieve certain citizens of Arkansas who purchased school lands," passed March 4, 1867, are hereby confirmed, ratified and made valid, and full faith and credit shall be given to said patents, deeds and official acts in all the courts of this state. *Provided*, Nothing herein shall be construed to prevent the setting aside of any of said deeds or patents for actual fraud or mistake.

SEC. 7136. Any right, title or interest which the state of Arkansas may have acquired, or holds by virtue of any judgment, decree, execution or sale of any court in this state, in lands for which patents or deeds have been made and issued

---

(*hh*.) See section 7138.
sec. 2.

as mentioned in section 7135, is hereby vested in the proper owners thereof under such deeds or patents.

SEC. 7137. The attorney representing the state of Arkansas is hereby instructed and required to dismiss all suits now pending for school lands where patents or deeds have been made therefor, as specified in section 7135, or if it does not appear on the face of the pleadings filed that such patents or deeds have been made, then the patent or deed may be pleaded in bar of the suit, or the court may dismiss the suit on exhibition and profert of such deed or patent; and where judgment or decree have been entered, and sale has not been made, the state's attorney shall enter satisfaction in full thereof on the presentation to him of such deed or patent.

SEC. 7138. If any purchaser of school lands shall have paid the purchase money thereof, and received no deed or patent therefor, or if any person now owing for school lands bought shall hereafter pay out his indebtedness therefor, and shall produce to the commissioner of state lands satisfactory evidence of such payment, the commissioner of state lands is authorized and required to execute to such person, or to his legal representative, a deed conveying all the right, title and interest of the state of Arkansas in such lands; but if payment has not been made before suit is begun, the purchaser shall also pay the costs of the suit. *Act December 14, 1875, as amended by act March 31, 1885, sec. 18, and act of February 16, 1885, sec. 2.*

LEASE OF SCHOOL LANDS.

SEC. 7139. All school lands in any county in this state susceptible of cultivation shall be leased by the county collector of said county from the first to the tenth of January in each year. *Act April 12, 1869, sec. 12.*

SEC. 7140. The manner and terms of leasing said lands shall be by public outcry to the highest bidder, the lessee paying one-half the amount of rent in cash at the time of leasing and the balance at the end of the year. *Ib.*

SEC. 7141. At least twenty days' public notice of the time and place of offering such lands for rent or lease shall be given by said collector by publishing the same in the newspapers of the county and by posting up hand-bills at the most prominent points throughout the county. *Ib.*

SEC. 7142. If any school lands offered for rent or lease at the time and in the manner above indicated shall not bring such price as the collector shall think a reasonable rent therefor, he shall be authorized to rent the same by private contract for the ensuing year, or for a longer term if he shall deem it expedient. *Ib.*

SEC. 7143. The occupants of school lands prior to the passage of this act shall be required to pay a reasonable annual rental during the time said lands had been so occupied. *Ib.*

SEC. 7144. The lessees of school lands shall be subject to the same provisions governing the lessees of other property, *Provided*, It shall not be rented for a less amount than was offered at public sale. *Ib.*

ACT XXXVII.

AN ACT to amend section 3325 of Sandels & Hill's Digest of the Statutes of Arkansas.

SECTION
1. Amends section 3325. County treasurers not to deduct commissions from same fund more than once.
2. Repeals all laws in conflict.
3. Act takes effect and in force from passage.

Be it enacted by the General Assembly of the State of Arkansas:

SECTION 1. That section 3325 of Sandels & Hill's Digest of the statutes of this state be and the same is hereby amended so as to read as follows: He shall be allowed, as commissions on the aggregate amount of all the school funds of the county coming into his hands in any one year, the rate of two per cent. and no more; *Provided*, That if any county treasurer shall have taken commissions from any particular school fund, the same fund shall not be subject to commissions in the hands of his successor in office.

SEC. 2. That all laws and parts of laws in conflict herewith be and the same are hereby repealed.

SEC. 3. That this act take effect and be in force from and after its passage.

Approved March 12, 1895.

OPINIONS.

OPINIONS.

APPLICATION OF FUNDS.

BY JONES.

I am, therefore, of opinion :

1. That the funds derived from the state and from the *per capita* tax, and from the tax voted by the district at the annual school meeting, after they reach the county treasury and are apportioned by the county court to the school district, become the absolute property of such district for the purpose of maintaining public schools therein, subject to disbursement on the warrant of the board of directors of a separate school district.

2. That, in other than separate school districts, the school directors may apply such funds to no other purpose than those directed by a majority of the electors of the district at their annual school meeting.

3. That, in other than separate school districts, the electors may, at their annual meeting, fix a site for the school house, or raise money for building or purchasing a school house ; *Provided*, The directors have given notice that these matters were to be submitted for consideration and action, as required by section 69 of the school law of December 7, 1875.

4. That it is within the power of the board of directors of separate school districts to apply any part of the fund belonging to such district, which has not been otherwise appropriated, to the purpose of building and purchasing a school house, irrespective of the source from which such fund came ; but that such power cannot be exercised by the

directors of other school districts, unless they have been authorized to do so by the electors of the district at an annual school meeting. See *School Act of December 7, 1875; Lee v. Trustees of School District 36 ; New Jersey Equity Reports, 581 ; Sandels & Hill's Digest, chapter 139.*

NOTE.—Most of the following opinions were made before the publication of Sandels & Hill's Digest, and the sections are changed to correspond with those in that digest.

RIGHTS OF PUPILS AS TO ADMISSION INTO PUBLIC SCHOOLS.

BY JONES.

I have the honor to acknowledge receipt of your communication of the 7th inst., in which you ask my opinion as to the legality and binding force of the following resolution, adopted by the board of directors of the school district of Prescott, to-wit:

Resolved, That such children only are entitled to admission as pupils in the Prescott free school as were residing in the school district of Prescott on the first day of the preceding September, and if names of such pupils do not appear in the enumeration, application for admission must first be made to the school board; *Provided*, That children of *bona fide* residents who may attain to the school age during the year may be admitted to the school.

The latter clause of section 7101, Sandels & Hill's Digest, reads as follows: " The board," referring to the board of directors of single school districts, " may make rules and regulations for their own government, and for the dispatch and regulation of the school business and affairs of the district not inconsistent with law."

The supreme court of Iowa, in the case of *Burdick v. Babcock, 31 Iowa, 362, 365*, in speaking of certain rules adopted by the board of directors of a school district by which certain pupils were suspended from the school for absence and tardiness, says: "Any rule of the school, not subversive of the rights of the children or parents, or in conflict with humanity and the precepts of divine law, which intends to advance the object of the law in establishing public schools, must be considered reasonable and proper."

So, in this case, the single question seems to me to be: Is the regulation of the Prescott board subversive of the rights of the children and parents, or in conflict with humanity and the precepts of divine law, and does it tend not to advance the object of the law in establishing public schools? If not, then it is unreasonable and improper, and can not be enforced. And this is the question to be determined and should be determined, as I conceive, by ascertaining as nearly as possible the spirit and intention of the legislature in dividing the counties into school districts, and investing each of such districts with certain powers to be exercised independently of others, and the scope and extent of such powers.

We find article 14 of the constitution of this state, section 3, that it is made the duty of the general assembly to provide by general laws for the support of common schools by taxes, not to exceed in any one year two mills on the dollar on the taxable property of the state; and by an annual *per capita* tax of one dollar, to be assessed on every male inhabitant of this state over the age of twenty-one years. This much is imperative on the general assembly; but the same section provides that "the general assembly may, by general law, authorize school districts to levy, by a vote of the qualified electors of such district, a tax not to exceed five mills on the dollar in any one year for school purposes; *Provided, further,* That no such tax shall be appropriated to any other purpose, nor to any other district than that for which it was levied."

Thus, we see, school districts are recognized by the constitution, and they are put beyond the power of the legislature, so far as the levying taxes for school purposes within their respective limits is concerned, and such tax can only be levied by the vote of the electors of the district (*Cole v. Blackwell 38 Ark., 271*); and can be appropriated to no other purpose, nor to any other district than that for which it was levied. The legislature is only authorized to confer upon the districts the power to levy such tax, but can not compel the levy. This power has been conferred, and each district is made a body corporate, capable of suing and being sued, contracting and being contracted with, acquiring and holding property, etc., etc., etc.

Section 7113, *ib.*, makes the provisions of the general school laws of the state, so far as applicable and not inconsistent or repugnant with the provisions of the special act for the regulation of public schools in cities and towns, apply to districts organized under said special act. Under the general school laws we find that the directors of each district shall annually, between the first and tenth days of September, transmit to the county examiner a written report of names and ages of all persons between the ages of six and twenty-one years residing in their district on the first day of September (*sec. 7077, ib.*); that the county examiner shall make a similar report to the superintendent of public instruction on or before the twentieth day of September (*secs. 7020 and 7023, ib.*); and to the county clerk of his county between the tenth and twentieth of September (*ib., sec. 6995*), which shall be laid by the county clerk before the county court (*ib., sec. 6996*); and that the county court shall distribute the distributive share of the county apportioned by the superintendent to the several districts in proportion to the number of persons within school age, respectively (*ib., sec. 6993*).

We further find that the directors " shall submit to the district, at the annual meeting, an estimate of the expenses of the district for that year, including the expenses of the school for the term of three months for the next year, after deducting the probable amount of school moneys to be apportioned to the district for that school year, and shall also submit an estimate of the expenses per month of continuing the school beyond the term of three months, and of whatever else may be necessary for the comfort and advancement of said school" (*ib.*, *sec. 7049*). And it is upon this report that the qualified electors, at their annual school meeting, act, when they determine the amount of taxes to be raised out of the district for the support of its schools.

The qualified electors of each district select the directors, who are entrusted with the management of the school affairs, and who in that capacity act as the representatives of the electors.

From all these provisions of the constitution and laws of the state, it seems apparent to me to be the policy of our state, that each school district should have the care and management of its entire school interests, independent of any control except the limitations prescribed by the law. How, it may well be asked, can a district provide the necessary means to carry on its schools, when persons outside of the district, who have contributed nothing towards the support or maintenance of the schools, shall have the absolute right to bring their children within the district, after the time for enumeration has passed, and compel their admission to the school as a matter of right? If it may be done by one person, it may be done by a thousand, or more; the principle is the same. And thus we may find a school district which has only provided the means necessary to support its own children—and this is all it can be required to do—forced to take into its schools other children for whom no provision has, or can be, made during the scholastic year, and without the power to provide adequate means for such a contingency. It could only result in disaster to the entire school interests of the district, which could certainly never have been within the contemplation of the law-makers.

The county court is empowered by the law to transfer children from one district to another (*ib., sec. 7062*). But in every such case tax of such children, levied by the district from which they were transferred, goes with them, and is used for their education (*ib., secs. 7063 and 7064*). Why does the law make such provisions, if it be true that the right exists without such exercise of authority by the county court? The very fact of the law making such provisions is evidence of the fact that the right does not otherwise exist.

The regulation of the Prescott school board does not absolutely exclude from the district school the children whose names fail to appear on the enumeration list, but it merely requires such children to make application to the board for admission before they shall be entitled to enter the school. By this means the board can judge whether such children should or should not be admitted. If it should act arbitrarily or unjustly, and refuse admission to one lawfully entitled, the law has provided an ample remedy for such cases. By the regulation the board can protect the district against imposition and fraud, and the better advance the objects for which free schools were organized.

I am, therefore, of the opinion that the regulation of the Prescott school board, above set forth, is reasonable and proper, and may be enforced

BY JONES.

Directors may not exclude children from any school to which they are lawfully entitled to admission.

In answer to your communication of this date, in which you ask my opinion upon the question, "whether the children of school age of parents who have become *bona fide* residents of a school district since the last enumeration are entitled to admission into the public schools of the district free of charge," I have the honor to say that I am of opinion that they are so entitled.

This opinion is not at all at variance with my opinion to you, of date March 10, 1885, contained in my biennial report to the governor in December, 1886, at page 72 *ab seq*. By reference to that opinion, it will be seen the question presented to me was whether a certain regulation adopted by the board of directors of the school district of Prescott was legal and binding. The regulation was as follows:

"*Resolved*, That such children are only entitled to admission as pupils in the Prescott free school as were residing in the school district of Prescott on the first day of the preceding September, and if names of such pupils do not appear in the enumeration, application for admission must first be made to school board. *Provided*, The children of *bona fide* residents who may attain to the school age during the year may be admitted to the school."

In the conclusion of that opinion, I said: "The regulation of the Prescott school board does not absolutely exclude from the district school the children whose names fail to appear on the enumeration list, but it merely requires such children to make application to the board for admission before they shall be entitled to enter the school. By this means the board can judge whether they should or should not be admitted. If it should act arbitrarily or unjustly, and should refuse admission to one lawfully entitled, the law has provided an ample remedy for such cases. By the regulation, the board can protect the district from imposition and fraud, and to better advance the objects for which free schools were organized."

The question now presented by you does not relate to the power of such boards to make regulations and rules for their own government, and for the dispatch and regulation of the school business and affairs of the district, not inconsistent with law. Such power is vested in them by the statute (*Di*-

gest, sec. 7101); but it is whether they can exclude from the public schools any child who is lawfully entitled to admission. This they cannot do.

Directors should remember that the right to attend school grows out of *bona fide* residence and not from an enumeration in a district or the payment of taxes. When a man moves into a district with the intention of making it his permanent residence, he acquires the right to send to the public schools at once. The directors are to decide from all the circumstances whether the residence is permanent or temporary. If temporary no free school privileges obtain.—[SUPERINTENDENT.

BY JONES.

Power of county court to fill vacancies in office of county examiner:

You refer me to section 7000, Sandels & Hill's Digest, requiring the county court of each county, at the first term thereof after each general election, to appoint a county examiner, and ask my opinion as to the power of the county court to make such appointment at any other time when a vacancy occurs in the office of county examiner. In reply I will say, that the matter of making such appointments being invested in the county court, it certainly has the power to fill any vacancy which may occur, but the tenure of office of such appointee will expire at the first term of the county court which shall be held after the next general election, when another appointment must be made.

BY JONES.

School directors may not teach in their own districts:

I have the honor to acknowledge receipt of your communication of the 3d instant, in which you ask my opinion upon the following questions:

"First—Can a school director be legally employed to teach in the public schools of his own district?

"Second—If not, what remedy have the people, if the directors presist in employing one of their own number to teach?"

In reply :

The office of school director is one of trust. Previous to the passage of the present school law he was called a trustee. In many of the states such officers are still called trustees. It is, however, immaterial whether the name be director or trustee, the office is one purely of trust and confidence, and the person filling it is governed by the same rules of law which govern other trustees, in so far as not to be allowed to make any profit from his office. It is a well settled rule that a trustee cannot use the trust property, nor his relation to it, for his own personal advantage. All the power and influence which the possession of a trust fund gives must be used for the advantage and profit of the beneficial owners, and not for the personal gain and emolument of the trustee. No other rule would be safe.

By examination of the school law it will be seen that the powers of the director are very large, and for the failure to perform, or for neglect of any duties of his office, he is liable to forfeit to his district the sum of twenty-five dollars.

Among his duties he is required to visit the schools at least once each term, and encourage the pupils in their studies, and give such advice to the teacher as may be for the benefit of teacher and pupils.

By other sections of the law it will be seen what the duties of the teachers are, and that it would be inconsistent with those duties for him to be a director. In fact, if a director were allowed to be a teacher in his own district, he would have to make a contract with himself, and would be using his position of trust for his own emolument and gain. This cannot be legally done.

I am, therefore, of opinion, in answer to your first question, that a school director cannot be legally employed to teach the public schools of his own district.

As to your second question, if the directors persist in employing one of their own number to teach, the people of the district can obtain redress through the courts to prevent such an abuse of power. They can be enjoined from doing so.

BY JONES.

Clerks may not charge fees for performing the duties required of them under the common school laws.

In answer to your inquiry, "Are county clerks entitled to ask, demand or receive fees from the several school districts in their respective counties for performing the duties required of them under the common school laws of the state—such, for instance, as filing reports of organization, of elections, of levy of school tax, of apportionment of common school funds, or any other duty enjoined upon them by said law?" I have the honor to say that the fees for clerks are regulated by statute in this state, and that unless the statute fixes a compensation for any particular service required of that officer, he is not entitled to ask, demand or receive any for the performance of it. See *Cole v. White County, 32 Ark., 45*.

By examination of the common school laws of this state, it will be observed that there is no compensation provided for the services required by the county clerks; consequently they are not entitled to fees for such services.

This is not a new question by any means, but has been frequently passed upon by the courts of the various states and by the English courts. From these decisions it may be considered as established law that where the law imposes a duty upon an officer he cannot claim a remuneration for fulfilling it unless the law has expressly conferred such right.

I am, therefore, clearly of the opinion that clerks are not entitled to fees for services required to be performed by them under the common school laws of this state.

BY JONES.

A school director may not be elected by less than a majority vote.

In answer to your inquiry, I have the honor to state that all the powers vested in the electors of a school district, in their annual school meetings, must be exercised by a majority of the votes cast at such meetings, and that no power can be exercised by less than such majority. Consequently a director cannot be elected by less than a majority of the votes cast at the meeting.

BY JONES.

Separate schools must be maintained in every district for each race—directors have discretion but to maintain the schools.

I am in receipt of your communication of a late date, in which you say : " In a certain school district of this state there are seventy-five or more white children of school age and only four colored children of that age.

" In another school district there are seventy-five or more colored children of school age and only four white children of that age.

" I wish to know whether it is the duty of the school directors in the first mentioned district to provide a school for the four colored children, and in the second mentioned district for the four white children."

In reply:

Section 1, article 14, of the constitution of the state, is as follows:

" Section 1. Intelligence and virtue being the safeguards of liberty, and the bulwark of a free and good government, the state shall ever maintain a general, suitable and efficient system of free schools, whereby all persons in the state between the ages of 6 and 21 years, may receive gratuitous instruction."

In compliance with this mandate of the constitution, the general assembly has prepared a system of free schools, one provision of which is as follows:

"The said board [of directors] shall make provisions for establishing separate schools for white and colored children and youths, and shall adopt such other measures as they may judge expedient for carrying the free-school system into effectual and uniform operation throughout the state, and providing, as nearly as possible, for the education of every youth." See *sec. 7041.*

The constitution of California, upon the subject of education, is similar to ours. The legislature of that state enacted that the education of children of African descent, and Indian children, shall be provided for in separate schools. In the case of *Ward v. Flood, 48 Cal. Rep., 36,* it is decided that it is clearly within the power of the legislature to enact such a law, and that a colored child may be excluded from a white school, and a white child from a colored school, where separate schools have been in fact established and maintained; but that "unless such separate schools be in fact maintained, all children of the school district, whether white or colored, have an equal right to become pupils at any common school organized under the laws of the state." To the same effect is the case of *State of, ex rel. Stoutmeyer, v. Duffy, 7 Nevada Rep., 342.*

In the case of *Maddox, et al., v. Neal, et al., 45 Ark. Rep., 121,* the supreme court of this state says: "A wide range of discretion is vested in these boards by the statute in the matter of the government and details of conducting the common schools, but in the nature of things, there is a limit to this discretion. Some positive and imperative duties are imposed upon them about which they have no discretion. The first and most important duty of the board is to make provisions for establishing schools. When the funds are provided, and the directors are not otherwise instructed by the school meeting of the district, the duty to provide a school for at least three months is mandatory, and the duty to establish separate schools for the whites and blacks is also incumbent on them. All the provisions of the law in relation to schools, in conformity to the constitutional mandate, are general, and the system, as far as the statute can make it, is uniform. No duty is imposed upon or discretion given to the directors about schools for one race that is not applicable to the other. It is the clear intention of the constitution and statutes alike to place means of education within the reach of every youth. Education at the public expense has become a legal right extended by the laws to all the people alike. No discrimination on account of nationality, caste or other distinction has been attempted by the law-making powers. The boards of directors are only the agents, the trustees appointed to carry out the system provided for. Their powers are no greater than the authority conferred by legislation. They can do nothing they are not expressly authorized to do, or which does not grow out of their expressed powers. * * * The opportunity of instruction in the public schools, given by the statute to all the youths of the state, is in obedience, as we have seen, to special command of the constitution, and it is obvious that a board of directors can have no discretionary power to single out a part of the children by the arbitrary standard of color, and deprive them of the benefits of the school privilege. To hold otherwise would be to set the discretion of the directors above all law."

It appears clear to me, from the authorities, and in view of the provisions of the constitution, and the statute above cited, that it is the duty of the directors of each school district to establish and maintain, with the funds at their disposal, separate schools for the white and colored children within their respective districts, so that every child of school age shall have the full benefit thereof; and I, therefore, conclude and so advise you, that this duty of directors is not limited by the number of children of either kind in the district, but applies to one child as well as to seventy-five or more.

NOTE.—This opinion represents the law as it stood at the time of its deliverance. Since then the legislature has authorized the transfer of the children of either race to adjoining districts where the number of either race in any district is ten or less. Now, if said transfer had been made then no school need be maintained. But where there are eleven or more children of either race they have the right to demand a school and it is the duty of the directors to maintain it out of the funds in their hands. See *sec.* 7062.

BY ATKINSON.

The treasurer of state to place the ten per cent. of the sales of all state lands to credit of school fund.

I am in receipt of your favor of the 15th inst., in which you ask my official opinion upon the following points, to-wit :

(1.) Has section 6932 of Sandels & Hill's Digest been repealed or amended?

(2) If not, who should place to the credit of the school fund " ten per cent. of the net proceeds of the sales of all state lands?"

(3.) How and by whom are the net proceeds determined?

In reply. I am of the opinion that the section of the digest mentioned by you has not been repealed or amended.

It seems to be the duty of the treasurer to keep books which shall show from whom moneys have been received by him and on what account. He is made the receiver of all public moneys not expressly required by law to be kept by some other person (see section 3255 of Sandels & Hill's Digest). I am of the opinion that the treasurer should place the funds mentioned to the credit of the common school fund. See *sec. 6139, Mansfield's Digest.*

Section 3210 of Mansfield's Digest makes it the duty of the commissioner of state lands to make a statement of the amount due or required by law for the purchase of state lands, in which he shall state concisely the particular matter or account for which said sum is to be paid, which is handed to the purchaser of state land and by him turned over to the treasurer. This would enable the latter officer to properly credit the funds received by him.

BY ATKINSON.

1. Every transferred person must pay the tax voted in the district to which he goes.

2. The tax which follows the person transferred is what he actually paid on his realty and personalty.

3. Nature of assessment.

Replying to your favor of the 26th inst., wherein you refer to me certain matters submitted by Duncan Flanagan, Esq., county judge of Clark county, relating to the construction of sections 7062-4 of Sandels & Hill's Digest, I have the honor to submit my opinion herewith.

You ask:

(1.) If a transfer of children be granted under section 7062, will the person applying for transfer pay the district school tax voted in the district from which he was transferred to the one in which his children have been transferred?

(2.) If he has real estate in several districts, will all or what part of the district tax follow the transfer?

(3.) In case of transfer, in what district must the real estate be assessed; and, if assessed in the district from which transfer is made, how can the district to which children have been transferred obtain the benefit of the tax?

The act of December 7, 1875, merely provided that "the district school tax" of the person whose children were transferred should be added to the school revenues of the district to which he had been transferred, and should not be included in the school revenues of the district wherein he remained. The difficulty under this law was, that a person might transfer his children to a district which levied a five-mill tax and get the benefit of this tax, while his property was taxed as belonging to the district in which he resided where he might vote "no tax," and, if a majority of the voters so voted, he would pay no tax. The tax was fixed by the district in which he resided, but was turned over to the district to which he was transferred when collected. This inequitable rule was intended to be changed by the act of March 30, 1883, and the more reasonable rule, "*Qui sentit commodum, sentire debet et onus,*" adopted. Although very obscurely drafted, the act sufficiently manifests an intention to transfer both the property and children to the district to which the tax-payer wishes to transfer for educational purposes. The act provides that the elector may vote in the district to which he had his children transferred. It is not to be supposed that he could vote there if his property was assessable in another district. The proviso that he could not vote outside of his political township was intended to prevent the act from being unconstitutional under section 1, of article 3, of constitution 1874. If he chose to remove his children and property out of his township and deprive himself of a right to vote in school elections, that was his own affair. "*Quilibet potest renunciare juri pro se introducto.*"

(1.) To your first question, therefore, I answer that a person obtaining a transfer of his property and children to an adjoining district will pay the district school tax voted by the district to which he has been transferred.

(2.) The law only provides that as to the district school tax, the property on which he paid in the district wherein he resides should be transferred to the district to which transfer of his children is made. This includes his tax on personalty and realty lying in that district only.

(3.) In case of transfer, the property is assessed as if in the district to which transfer is made. Section 7064, Sandels & Hill's Digest provides the way the accounts are to be kept where the districts are in two counties.

BY ATKINSON.

School boards must act as corporate bodies and separately as individuals.

You ask, "Can a majority of a board of directors of a school district bind the district by a contract for the employment of teachers, or for other purposes, without a full meeting of the board?"

This question has been frequently adjudicated by the courts of the different states. I have collected a few extracts from them, which I present you, viz.:

In *Herrington v. District, 47 Iowa, 13*, the court said " While it is true that a majority of the board will govern in the absence of a provision by statute, or in the articles of incorporation, requiring the concurrence of a greater number, yet their determination is valid only after the minority have had an opportunity to be heard. A board must act as a unit, and in the manner prescribed. The determination of the members individually is not the determination of the board. In *McCulloch v. Ross, 577, 5 Denio*, the court said : ' The concurrence of a majority of the board when duly assembled is requisite to constitute a valid act. The assent of the members separately is not enough.' "

In *Townsend v. School Trustees, 41 N. J. L., 313*, it was held :

" The duty of these trustees, in the selection of teachers, was not ministerial merely ; they were obliged to examine into the qualifications of teachers, and to exercise judgment and discretion in their selection; it was the performance of an important public duty, in the execution of which conference and comparison of judgments were necessary in reaching proper results. It was an act judicial in its nature, and the general rule governing such bodies so acting is, unless special provisions of the is otherwise made, that all must meet, or have notice to meet, when official action is intended." * * * * " It was clearly not the intention of the legislature, in the school law, to confer upon the individual members constituting the board of trustees the power of acting separately in the selection and appointment of teachers. The intention was to have them act and confer together, the result of their combined judgment, or of the majority of them, constituting a single act."

In the *State ex rel. v. Leonard, 3 Cooper's Ch., 179*, it is said:

"Neither the majority nor the whole of these had power individually to grant such permission. It could only be given by them when assembled as a board."

"It was evidently contemplated by the legislature that a school district should have the benefit to be derived from the united experience and wisdom of all the members of the board." *People v. Peters, 4 Neb., 254.*

In *Wilson v. Waltersville School District, 46 Conn., 407*, it was held:

"The rule of the common law undoubtedly is that public agents may act by majorities, provided all are present, or have proper notice, to be present.

"Their duties are important, and require the exercise of sound judgment and discretion, and their action in the employment of teachers may be attended with important consequences, both pecuniary and moral. When several persons are appointed it would seem to be for the very purpose of giving the district the benefit of the combined judgment and good sense of all."

I am of the opinion that the rules for the government of school boards, as promulgated in the foregoing decisions, are correct and proper, and should be recommended by you for the observance of those acting in that capacity in our state.

BY KINSWORTHY.

Junius Jordan, Superintendent of Public Instruction:

DEAR SIR—I have the honor to acknowledge receipt of your recent communication requesting me to answer the following question:

"When does a newly elected member of the board of directors of a special school district become an active member of the board?"

Answering this question, I have this to say :

Section 7091 of Sandels & Hill's Digest states that annually on the third Saturday in May, there shall be elected two directors who shall serve three years and until their successors are elected and qualified. This section does not state that said directors shall hold three years from the date of their election, but that they shall hold three years from the day they begin to serve.

Section 7098 of Sandels & Hill's Digest states : " Each person elected director shall take the oath of office within five days after receiving a certificate of election." While the directors are elected on the third Saturday in May, they are given five days from the date they receive their certificate of election in which to qualify; so if a director qualifies within the said five days his term of office would begin the day he qualifies and end three years from that day, provided his successor qualifies on or before that day.

I am, therefore, of the opinion that a newly elected director can be qualified as soon as he receives his certificate of election, but that his term of office would begin upon the day his predecessor's term of office expires, which day would be three years from the date he began to serve as director, provided that time was within five days after he received a certificate of election ; if not, his term of office would begin the fifth day after receiving his certificate of election.

In giving this opinion I have not been unmindful of section 7100 of the digest, for this section cannot change the provisions of the sections previously mentioned, as this section is a part of the act of 1885, and the above mentioned sections are a part of the act of 1893, so the latter act repeals the former act wherever and whenever they come in conflict.

Yours respectfully,   E. B. KINSWORTHY,
Attorney General.

APPENDIX.

APPENDIX.

FORMS FOR THE USE OF SCHOOL OFFICERS.
Form I. Examiner's Requisition Blank.

OFFICE OF COUNTY EXAMINER,

....

....18..........

To the State Superintendent of Public Instruction,
Little Rock, Ark.

SIR: The blanks and blank books needed for a proper administration of the public school affairs of this county are as follows:

	No. on Hand	No. Required
Examiner's Record		
Annual School Meeting Notices		
Directors' Estimates of District Expenses		
Certificate of Election of School Directors		
Certificates of Tax Levied		
Directors' Oaths		
Directors' Annual and Enumeration Reports		
Contracts between Directors and Teachers		
Directors' Warrant Books		
Examination Notices		
County Examiner's Annual Reports		
Teachers' Certificates		
Directors' Records		
Teachers' Registers		
School Laws		
County Institute Notices		
Poll-Books		
No. of School Districts in the County		

Directions for shipping the above.

....

....

....

Respectfully,

....
County Examiner.

S—9

Form II.

ANNUAL SCHOOL MEETING.

NOTICE.

There will be an Annual School Meeting of the Electors of School District No ....County, at ...., the third Saturday in May, 189.... At this meeting the following matters will be submitted to the consideration and action of the Electors of said District :

....
....
....

It is desired that every Elector be present.

....
....

Directors.

Date..189....

Directors will please bear in mind that this notice must be posted in three or more conspicuous places, at least fifteen days before the time of meeting, and that the objects of this meeting must be inserted in the appropriate blanks above, as provided for in section 7035 of the present School Law of Arkansas.

Form III.

DIRECTORS'
ESTIMATE OF DISTRICT EXPENSES.

Electors of School District No. .... *County of*
.... *State of Arkansas.*

We respectfully submit, in accordance with Section 7049 of the School Law, the following as our estimate of the expenses of the Public Schools in this District, for the term of three months during the present scholastic year, beginning the first of last July, and of the expenses per month of continuing the schools longer than three months.

AMOUNT NECESSARY.

For Teachers' Salaries ....
For Purchase or Lease of Sites. ....
For Purchase, Erection or Hire of Houses.. ....
For Repairs of Houses and Grounds.. ....
For Fuel and Incidental Expenses.. ....
For Furniture, Apparatus, Light, &c.. ....
For other purposes.. ....
        Total ....
Amount which we will probably receive from the State Apportionm't ....
Remainder to be raised by a District Tax ....
Expense for continuing the schools ....longer than
    three months, at ....dollars per month...............
Total amount to be raised by District Tax..

The above estimate is respectfully submitted for your consideration and action.

....
.... } Directors.
....

Dated, May........../.............................189......

Form IV.

CERTIFICATE OF ELECTION OF SCHOOL DIRECTORS.

STATE OF ARKANSAS, }
County of................................. }   SCHOOL DISTRICT No.........................

We hereby certify that at the Annual School Election held on the ....

day of May, 189 ....., ...

was elected School Director for the next ....years.

.... v ....

....

Judges.

This.............................. ....May, 189......

(See Section 7036, School Law.)

SCHOOL LAWS. 133

Form V.

CERTIFICATE OF JUDGES AND CLERKS OF SCHOOL ELECTION.

STATE OF ARKANSAS, ⎫
.... County, ⎬
District No. .... ⎭

We hereby certify that the election held on this day, in District No............................
....County, Arkansas, pursuant to law, the number of votes hereinafter mentioned were cast for the several persons named below for Directors, and for and against Tax, and amount of Taxes voted.

For Directors	No. Votes Received	For Tax	No. Votes Received	Mills
		Whole No. of Votes Cast		
		Whole No. of Votes Cast Against Tax		
		For Teachers' Salaries		
		For Purchasing or Lease of Houses		
		For Building or Repairing		
		For Furniture and Apparatus		

Given under our hands this.................day of ....A. D. 189.....
ATTEST:
....
....
Clerks.   Judges.

NOTE.—This form is a part of the poll book which is furnished by the examiner to each district.

Form VI.

DIRECTORS' OATH.

I,.., do solemnly swear (or affirm) that I will support the Constitution of the United States, and the Constitution of the State of Arkansas, and that I will faithfully discharge the duties of the office of Director of District No..upon which I am about to enter.

....

Post-office.......................... ....

   Sworn and subscribed to before me this.......:..........................:..... day of

      ....189.....

       ....County Clerk.

    See Section 7086, School Law.

SCHOOL LAWS. 135

Form VII.

ANNUAL REPORT

Of the Directors of School District No. .... to the County Examiner of .... County, Arkansas, for the last School Year, ending June 30, 189...., and the Enumeration Report of all persons between the ages of Six and Twenty-one Years, residing in District No. .... in .... County, Arkansas, on the first day of September, 189....

Pupils
- Enrollment
  - Number of pupils enrolled in the public schools ....
    - White, males ....
    - White, females ....
    - Colored, males ....
    - Colored, females ....
- Average Attendance
  - Average number in daily attendance ....
    - White, males ....
    - White, females ....
    - Colored, males ....
    - Colored, females ....
- Number pupils in private and denominational schools ....

Number of Pupils in Each Branch Taught
- Orthography ....
- Reading ....
- Mental Arithmetic ....
- Written Arithmetic ....
- English Grammar ....
- Geography ....
- Penmanship ....
- History ....
- Higher Branches ....

Teachers
- White
  - Name .... Salary per month $..........
  - Grade of License ....
  - Name .... Salary per month $..........
  - Grade of License ....
  - Name .... Salary per month $..........
  - Grade of License ....
  - Number of days the schools were taught ....
  - Number of visits received from the Directors ....
- Colored
  - Name .... Salary per month $..........
  - Grade of License ....
  - Name .... Salary per month $..........
  - Grade of License ....
  - Name .... Salary per month $..........
  - Grade of License ....
  - Number of days the schools were taught ....
  - Number of visits received from the Directors ....

Wages
- Total amount paid for schools—
  - From tax .... $..........
  - From subscription .... $..........

School Houses
- Entered during the year .... Cost $..........
- Whole number of public schools houses in dist. Value $..........
- Total value of public school houses ....
- Total value all other property belonging to district ....
- Condition of school house grounds ....
- Number school house grounds enclosed ....
- Number school house grounds not enclosed ....

FINANCIAL STATEMENT.

Receipts from all sources .... $..........
Disbursements .... $..........
Balance on hand June 30th .... $..........

SCHOOL LAWS.

Form VII—*Continued.*
ENUMERATION REPORT.

Enumeration of all persons between the ages of Six and Twenty-one years, residing in School District No. ....
in .... County, Ark., on the first day of September, 189....

No.	Name.	White.			Colored.		
		Age.	Male.	Female.	Age.	Male.	Female.

Name.	No.	Name of Parent or Guardian.	Post-Office.

DEAF, DUMB, BLIND AND INSANE UNDER THIRTY YEARS OF AGE.

Name.	Age.	Deaf, Dumb, Blind or Insane.	To What Extent.

SUMMARY OF ENUMERATION.

Total Number White Males ....
Total Number White Females ....
    Aggregate ....
Total Number Colored Males ....
Total Number Colored Females ....
    Aggregate ....
Total Aggregate ....
Total Number of Deaf ....
Total Number of Dumb ....
Total Number of Blind ....
Total Number of Insane ....

STATE OF ARKANSAS, } ss.
COUNTY OF .... }

We .... Directors of School District No. ...... County of ...., being duly sworn, state on oath that the foregoing report is in all respects a just and true statement of the names and ages of all children in District No. ...... in .... County, Arkansas, between the ages of Six and Twenty-one years, on September, 189..., and of the statistics, affairs and transactions in said district, for the time and as to the matters therein mentioned, according to the best of our knowledge and belief. So help us God.

.... 189........

.... Directors.

Subscribed and sworn to before me this .... day of .... J. P.

SCHOOL LAWS.   137

Form VIII.

TEACHER'S CONTRACT.

STATE OF ARKANSAS, } ss.
County of.................................

THIS AGREEMENT, between ....

....

as Directors of School District No.................in the County of............
State of Arkansas, and..
who agrees to teach a Common School in said District, is as follows:

The said Directors agree upon their part, in consideration of the covenants of said Teacher, hereinafter contained, to employ the said ....to teach a Common School in said District, for the term of ....months, commencing on the.....................day of.................................A. D. 189....., to pay therefor in the manner, and out of the funds provided by law, the sum of................................Dollars, for each school month.

Said Directors further agree that all the steps required or allowed by law to be taken by said District and its officers, to secure the payment of teachers' wages, shall be so had and taken promptly, and the requirements of the law in favor of the teacher, complied with by said District.

The Teacher, on ....part, agrees to keep............school open............hours each school day; keep carefully the Register required by law; preserve from injury to the utmost of............power the District property; give said school..................entire time and best efforts during the school hours; use.............utmost influence with parents to secure a full attendance of scholars, and generally to comply with all the requirements of the laws of this State in relation to Teachers to the best of............ability.

Signature—

....
....
....
                                                                    Directors.
....
                                                                    Teacher.

Date...................................189..... Place ....

(See Sections 7042 and 7043 of School Law.)

SCHOOL LAWS.

Form IX.

BLANK WARRANT.

No .... DISTRICT SCHOOL FUND, DISTRICT No.........,.......

....189.....

To Treasurer .... *County, Ark.:*

Pay to.............. ....or Order

the sum of... .... DOLLARS,.
                                                                                    100
for ...., out of the·

....*.*......Fund.

....
                                                Directors.

(See Sections 7051 and 7052 of School Law.)

Form X.

FOR PUBLIC EXAMINATIONS.

NOTICE.

Notice is Hereby Given that there will be a

PUBLIC EXAMINATION OF TEACHERS

At ....

the ....days

of ....A. D. 189 ....., to ascertain the

Professional Qualifications of all persons desiring to teach in the PUBLIC SCHOOLS

of .... County.

....
                                                County Examiner.

....County, Arkansas.

Date ....

(See Section 7009 of School Law.)

SCHOOL LAWS. 139

Form XI.

STATEMENT

OF THE PUBLIC SCHOOL FUNDS OF .... COUNTY, FOR THE YEAR ENDING JUNE 30, 189......

Amount Received.	U. S. Currency.	State Scrip.	Total.	Aggregate.
Balance on hand June 80, 189—................				
From Common School Fund (State)				
" District Tax..				
" Poll Tax...... ..../.....				
" Sale or Lease of Houses or Sites..				
" Grants or Gifts				
" Other Sources.............				
Total....				

Amount Expended.	U. S. Currency.	State Scrip.	Total.	
For Teachers' Salaries..				
" Purchasing Houses or Sites...................				
" Building and Repairing...				
" Purchasing Apparatus, etc.				
" Treasurer's Commissions				
" Other Purposes..				
Total...				

Balance in County Treasury Uuexpended.	U. S. Currency.	State Scrip.	Total.	
Of Common School Fund				
" District Fund				
" Funds from all other Sources				
Total...........				

STATE OF ARKANSAS, }
County of............... .... }

        I do hereby certify that the foregoing is a correct statement of the Public School Funds of..County, for the year ending June 30, 189 .....

                              .... ,................................. ......
                                               County Treasurer.

    Date....................................... ....

(See Section 7084 of School Law.)

140   SCHOOL LAWS.

FORM XII.

REQUIREMENTS—NOTHING BELOW FIFTY TO BE CONSIDERED.

For First Grade—Arithmetic, Grammar, Orthography, Eighty-five per cent each; Average of Eighty-five per cent in the remainder.
For Second Grade—Arithmetic, Grammar, Orthography, Seventy-five per cent each; Average of Seventy-five per cent in the remainder.
For Third Grade—Arithmetic, Grammar, Orthography, Sixty per cent each; Average of Sixty per cent in the remainder.

DEPARTMENT OF PUBLIC INSTRUCTION,
STATE OF ARKANSAS,
TEACHER'S LICENSE

No........   Grade No........

THIS IS TO CERTIFY, That................having presented satisfactory testimonials of good moral character, has this day been examined in Orthography, Reading, Writing, Mental and Written Arithmetic, English Grammar, Modern Geography, History of the United States, Theory and Practice of Teaching, Physiology and Hygiene, and the UNITED STATES System of Land Survey, and is hereby LICENSED to teach the same in the PUBLIC SCHOOLS OF THIS STATE, within the limits of................ County, for the term of................ year................ months from the date hereof, unless sooner revoked.

GIVEN UNDER MY HAND, This................ day of................ A. D. 189....

....
COUNTY EXAMINER.

STANDING—ONE HUNDRED BEING TAKEN AS THE STANDARD OF PERFECTION.

Orthography........ Writing........ Mental Arithmetic........ Modern Geography........
Reading........ English Grammar........ Written Arithmetic........ History of the U. S........
U. S. System of Land Survey........ Theory and Practice........ Physiology........

Form XIII.

CERTIFICATE OF SCHOOL TAX LEVIED.
ARKANSAS.

Office of School Directors, District No. ....

....189.......

TO THE HONORABLE COUNTY COURT

   of..*County, State of Arkansas:*

We hereby certify that at a meeting of the voters of School District No. ....
in...................................County, held on the...............day of.......................189........
it was voted that the following number of mills...
be levied on the taxable property in said District, for the following school purposes, to-wit:

Expense of Teachers,	....................Mills.
Purchase or Lease of Site,	....................Mills.
Purchase, Erection or Hire of House,	....................Mills.
Repair of House and Grounds,	....................Mills.
Fuel,	....................Mills.
Furniture,	....................Mills.
Other Purposes, {	....................Mills.
....	....................Mills.
Total Amount..	....................Mills.

And your Honorable Body will please levy a tax on the taxable property of this District equal to the above total amount, in accordance to law.

....

Attest:

....
                                                                Directors.
....
              Chairman.

   Dated this...................day of...............................189......

Form XIV.

NOTICE OF COUNTY INSTITUTE.

Office of COUNTY EXAMINER,

.... *189....*

BOARD OF DIRECTORS, DISTRICT NO.................

You will notify all Teachers holding Certificates of Qualification to teach in Public Schools, that a Teachers' Institute will be held at...

........................on the...... ....

·days of .... 189 .....

Also that Section 7073 as amended of the School Law requires their attendance.

Urge upon them the importance of attending.

Very Respectfully,

....
County Examiner.

SCHOOL LAWS.   143

Form XV.

OATH OF JUDGES

OF SCHOOL ELECTION.

STATE OF ARKANSAS, }
County of .... }

We,..
and .... do swear that we will perform the duties of Judges of this election according to law, and to the best of our abilities, and that we will studiously endeavor to prevent fraud, deceit and abuse in conducting the same, and that we will not disclose how any elector shall have voted, unless required to do so as witnesses in a judicial proceeding, or a proceeding to contest an election.

....
....
....
                                                            Judges.
....

Form XVI.

OATH OF CLERKS

OF SCHOOL ELECTION.

STATE OF ARKANSAS, }
County of .... }

We,..
and..do swear that we will perform the duties of Clerks of this election to the best of our abilities; and that we will faithfully record the names of all voters; and that we will not disclose how any elector shall have voted, unless required to do so as witnesses in a judicial proceeding, or a proceeding to contest an election.

....
....
                                                            Clerks.
....

I DO CERTIFY, that ....
and..Judges, and..
....and..
Clerks, of the election held in District No................... on the .... day of....................... 189...., were severally sworn as the law directs, previous to entering upon their respective duties.
        Given under my hand as such......................this............day of.......................189....
....

(NOTE—Forms V, XV and XVI are parts of poll-book.)

INDEX.

A

ANNUAL SCHOOL MEETING: PAGE.
    How constituted 42, 82
    Who may vote 42
    Quorum 42, 84
    Powers of 42, 43, 44, 45, 82
    Who to hold 46, 82
    Ballot 46
    How to count the votes 46
    Duties of county court 47

APPARATUS:
    What amount may be expended for 55
    To be approved by whom 55

APPORTIONMENT:
    By superintendent 19
    By county court 27, 28, 29, 90
    Basis of 27, 19

ATTESTATION:
    Of reports 61

AUDITOR:
    Duties of concerning common school fund 13
    Superintendent of public instruction has access to books of .. 20

ATTORNEY GENERAL (*See Opinions*):
    Duties of as to common school fund 14, 97
    Opinion of, when given 20
    Opinion of .... 107 *et seq.*

AUTHENTICATION:
    Of any paper or document 22

B

BLANKS:
    Forms of .... 129 *et seq.*
    To be furnished by state superintendent 16

INDEX.

BRANCHES:
    For state certificate.. 21
    For county certificate 36, 37, 140
    For county examiner's certificate............................ 32

BOOKS:
    List of prepared by superintendent........................... 22
    To be adopted by directors 55

BOOK AGENTS:
    State superintendent not to act as........................... 21
    County examiner not to act as................................ 21

BOUNDARY LINES:
    Of school districts changed by court......................... 26

BUILDINGS:
    Report to be made of... 62
    Care of, in whose hands...................................... 51
    Site for, how designated..................................... 43

C

COMMON SCHOOL (*See Free School*):
COMMON SCHOOL FUND (*See Free School Fund*):
    Collection of.....................................11, 12, 13, 97
    No cost where plaintiff is unsuccessful...................... 13
    Whence received..................................11, 12, 13
    Debts due... 13, 97
    County treasurers' commission on............................ 102

COLLECTORS:
    Duties of as to *per capita* tax............................. 13

COMMISSIONERS, COMMON SCHOOL....................13 *et seq.*
    How composed... 13
    Time and place of meeting.................................... 13
    Who presides... 14
    The secretary of... 14
    Record of.. 14
    General duties of.. 14, 15

CORPOREAL PUNISHMENT..........................66 *et seq.*

COUNTY CLERKS:
    Duties of.................................20, 29, 32, 116

COUNTY COURT:
    Apportionment by.............................12, 27, 29
    Change of districts....................................... 24, 25
    To appoint county examiners.................................. 30

INDEX.   iii

COUNTY EXAMINER (*see examiner*)..........................30 *et seq*
CERTIFICATES:
    State.. 21
    County, form of..23, 140
    Requirements 36, 37
    Revocation of.. 36, 37
CHARTS.. 55
COUNTY, NEW, Etc.. 30
CONTRACTS GENERALLY 52, 53, 54, 57, 58, 59
CLERK BOARD OF DIRECTORS......................43, 46, 60

D

DISTRICTS........................10, 12, 24, 25, 26, 27, 88, 89
    Dissolution of 25
    Boundaries of 24, 25
    Changes of...24, 25, 26
    Style and name of.. 25
    Powers of.. 26
    New districts..26, 29
    Special or separate districts..............................81 *et seq.*
    Transfers from one to another.........................70, 71, 72
    Vacancy in office of.....................................49, 83
    Rights of parties... 72
    Must be numbered.....................................40, 41
    Inhabitants of to be encouraged, how...................38, 39
    May be dissolved by county court 24
DIRECTORS..47 *et seq.*
    Become active members of board when..................124, 125
    How elected......................................43, 47, 81, 82
    Cannot be elected without majority vote...............116, 117
    Duties of.......................................48-73, 84, 85, 86
    May not be county examiners............................ 32
    When to qualify...48, 84
    Who to administer....................................... 48
    Penalty for refusing to serve............................48, 49
    Penalty for non-performance of duty 49, 73
    Penalty for failure to report tax......................... 73
    Vacancy, how filled....................................49, 83
    Must establish separate schools.......................... 49
    Must act as corporate bodies 122, 123, 124
    Have general charge 50, 51, 85
    Must contract with teachers..........................52, 53, 85

INDEX.

DIRECTORS—*Continued.*

    Must adopt text books: 55
    Must furnish register 55
    Must visit the schools 55, 56, 90
    Must submit estimate 56, 57
    Must defend for district 59
    Must draw orders on treasurer 59, 88
    Must not teach in their own districts 114, 115
    Must close schools on examination days 72, 76
    Duties as to notices 36, 59, 60
    Duties of clerk of board 60, 88
    Must report to county clerk 61
    Must report to county examiner 61
    Must settle with county treasurer 62
    May permit elder persons to attend 70
    May suspend pupils .... 63 *et seq.*
    Duties as to rules .... 63 *et seq.*
    Duties as to transferred children 71
    Duties as to private schools 72
    Exempt from working roads 72, 73
    Penalty for failure to report tax levied 73
    For separate school districts .... 81 *et seq.*

DISBURSEMENT OF FUNDS 79
DECISIONS .... 107 *et seq.*
DISTURBANCE OF SCHOOL 78
DICTIONARIES 55

E

ELECTION:

    School 42, 81, 82
    Who may vote 42
    How to organize 42, 43, 46
    What may be done at 42, 43, 44, 45, 46
    Who to hold 46
    Time for opening and closing poles 46
    Form of ballots 46
    Who to count 46
    Duties of election judges 46, 47, 82
    Duty of county clerk 46, 47
    Duty of county court 46, 47
    In separate school districts 81, 82
    Majority to elect 116, 117

INDEX. v

ELECTORS:
    Must have pole tax receipt.................................... 42
    Powers of...................................... 42, 43, 44, 45
    When to meet...................................... 42
ENFORCEMENT:
    Of rules.................................... 63 et seq.
ENUMERATION:
    Report of.................................... 61, 62, 63
EXAMINATIONS:
    Must be public and quarterly........................... 33, 35, 36
    Only teachers deserving license must teach............. 76
    Private 38, 39
    Re-examination.................................... 35, 36
    Schools must be closed 72
    Not to be held at time of institute 76
    Teachers not to be charged for loss of time............ 76
EXAMINERS:
    Appointment of.................................... 30
    Duties of clerk 32
    Duties of judge.................................... 30, 31
    Duties of state superintendent.................... 32
    Examination of.................................... 32
    Examination a personal service............ 33, 34, 35
    Expenses of.................................... 41
    General duties of.................................... 31 et seq.
    How removed.................................... 41
    Institutes must be held by 76
    May appoint deputy.................................... 41
    May not be a director.................................... 32
    Must hold public quarterly examinations............ 35
    Must present expense account.................... 41
    Must keep record of licensed teachers............ 38
    Must prepare a report.................................... 29, 40
    Must number school districts.................... 40
    Must encourage the people.................................... 38, 39
    Penalties for failure to perform his duties......... 41
    Qualifications.................................... 33
    Reports to county clerk.................................... 29
    Revocation of license.................................... 36, 37
    Salary of.................................... 33, 41
    What to examine.................................... 36, 37
    When to examine.................................... 33, 35

EXAMINERS—*Continued*.

    When to qualify.. 32
    Who are excluded from examinations........................ 36
    Who may be cited to be re-examined......................... 36
    Vacancy in office of... 114

ESTIMATE:

    Of school directors................................... 56, 57, 58

EXEMPTIONS:

    From road duty... 72, 73

FEES:

    Exaction of.................................... 86, 87, 116
    Of justice of the peace and other officers.................. 13
    Exaction of..................................... 86, 87
    Of surveyor.. 94
    Of clerks................................... 82, 95, 116
    Of county examiners.. 32, 33

FORMS:

    For use of school officers............................... 129 *et seq.*

FREE SCHOOLS:

    Definition of... 10
    High schools may be..................................... 11, 88
    Failure of county to receive school fund..................... 30
    Fund, common school......................... 11, 12, 13, 102
    Claims due, how collected................................ 13, 97
    Limit of taxes for... 9, 47
    Per capita tax for... 9, 12
    Power to tax for.. 10
    Right to attend....................................... 9, 63, 70
    Support of... 9, 10
    What may be taught in................................... 37, 77

FUNDS:

    Common school............................. 11, 12, 13, 102
    Treasurers to report..................................... 79, 80
    Treasurers' commission on.................................. 102
    To be invested.. 14
    How apportioned...................................... 19, 27, 90
    How paid out of state treasury.............................. 20

G

GLOBES.. 55
GRADES OF CERTIFICATES................................ 21, 22, 37

H

HIGH SCHOOLS MAY BE SUPPORTED BY TAXATION.......11, 85, 86

I

INSTITUTES:
    State Superintendent to hold............................... 16
    County examiner to hold................................... 76
    Not to be held at time of examination..................... 76
    Teachers must attend...................................... 76
    County Normal Institute................................... 23
INCOMPETENCY OF TEACHERS............................. 37, 87

J

JUDGE, COUNTY (*See County Court*):......................... 12, 30

L

LAND SURVEY, ETC.:
    Required to be taught.................................... 37
LEASE OF SCHOOL LANDS................................101, 102
LICENSE, COUNTY... 37
    Unlawful without examination.............................. 38
    State, requirements for................................... 21

M

MONTH:
    Term defined.. 54
MAPS.. 55
MAYOR:
    Duties of in separate districts........................... 81
MEMORIAL:
    House No. 1.. 96
NORMAL SCHOOLS:
    Power to support by taxation............................. 11
    County normal institutes................................. 23
    Teachers must attend..................................... 76
    Length of county normal.................................. 24
    District normals... 24
NOTICE:
    Of annual school meeting................................. 59, 60
    Of petition for transferred children..................... 71
    Of county examiners...................................... 36, 76
    Of change in district.................................... 25
    For separate districts................................... 81, 83

O

OFFICE OF STATE SUPERINTENDENT..................... 16
OATH OF OFFICE.......... ....32, 48, 84
OFFICERS:
    Election of, how certified.............. 61
OPINIONS OF ATTORNEY GENERAL:
    Application of funds...107, 108
    As to clerk's fees..... 116
    As to separate schools...........................117, 118, 119, 120
    Directors must receive a majority..... .... 116, 117
    Directors serve, how long....:............................124, 125
    Duties of treasurer...................................... 120
    Duties of transferred persons............................121, 122
    Power of court to fill vacancy............................. 114
    Rights of pupils...... ....108—113
    School boards, corporate bodies................... ....122, 123, 124
    School directors as teachers........................ ....114, 115
    Directors become active members when......................124, 125

P

PUBLIC SCHOOL (*See Free School*):
    Private schools can not be based upon public taxation........... 10
PROSECUTING ATTORNEY:
    Duties of as to school fund............................... 14, 80
PERMANENT SCHOOL FUND.. 12
PENALTIES..................................41, 48, 49, 62, 73, 78, 79
PRIVATE SCHOOL............................... ....,......... 72
    No taxation for support of 10
POLL BOOKS:
    To be used by directors in annual meeting..................... 17
PATENTS...99, 100, 101
PETITION:
    For separate school.. 81
    For transfer..70, 71
PUNISHMENT... 66

Q

QUESTIONS:
    To be furnished by State Superintendent............ 16

R

RACES, SEPARATE SCHOOLS FOR.................................. 49, 71
RIGHTS:
    Of district over funds.. 28
    Of parties transferred.....................................72, 121, 122
    Of pupils into public schools 108, 109, 110, 111, 112, 113, 114
REGISTERS:
    Form of.. 25
    Who to furnish.. 16, 25
    Directors must procure... 55
    Teachers' duties.. 75, 77
RE-EXAMINATIONS:
    Required... 35, 38
    Renewals of certificates... 38
REVOCATION OF LICENSE... 36, 37
RECORDS:
    Of state supnrintendent... 16
REPORT:
    Of state superintendent... 17
    Of county examiner.. 40
    Of school directors to county examiners........................... 61, 62
    Of school directors to county clerk................................... 61
REMOVAL:
    Of teacher.. 37, 87
    Of county examiner... 41
RULES:
    What may be prescribed by State Superintendent..................... 16
    Of directors and teachers......................................63 et seq.

S

SEAL OF STATE SUPERINTENDENT...................................... 22
SECRETARY OF STATE:
    One of board of commissloners....................................... 13
    Shall be president of board.. 14
    May call meeting of board.. 13, 14
SEPARATE SCHOOL DISTRICTS...................................81 et seq.
SEPARATE SCHOOLS:
    For both races... 49, 71, 120
SALARY OF EXAMINERS.. 32, 41
SCHOOL DIRECTORS (*see directors*)............................47 et seq.
SCHOOL DISTRICTS (*see districts*).............................24 et seq.

INDEX.

SCHOOL LANDS..91 et seq.
SCHOOLS FOR CITIES AND TOWNS.......................81 et seq.
SCHOOL HOUSES:
    Tax must be voted for.. 43, 44
    Director to have charge of and contract for................... 51, 55
    Not lawful to fix a site for, or vote tax for, when............... 60
    Private school may be taught in................................. 72
SCHOOL LAWS:
    State superintendent to publish................................. 20
SECTARIAN BOOKS PROHIBITED..................................... 77
SIXTEENTH SECTIONS..........................12, 91, 92, 93, 94, 96
SPECIAL SCHOOL DISTRICT.....................................81 et seq.
STUDIES:
    Report of... 61
SUITS AT LAW:
    Direcrors duties... 59
STATISTICS... 19
STATE SUPERINTENDENT OF PUBLIC INSTRUCTION:
    Duties of with reference to common school fund........14, 17, 18
    Apportionment by... 19, 21
    General duties of....................................... 13 et seq.
    To publish laws and render decisions........................... 20
    Vacancy in office.. 21
    Not to act as agent.. 21
    To grant state certificats..................................... 21
    To recommend books, etc.................................. 22, 55
    Must examine county examiner.................................. 32
SUPERVISION OF PUBLIC SCHOOLS:
    To whom confined.. 15, 16
STATE LANDS, TEN PER CENT OF SALES......................11, 120
SUSPENSION:
    Power of... 63

T

TAXATION FOR SCHOOLS..........................9, 10, 11, 46, 47
    For normal and high schools................................... 11
TEACHERS' INSTITUTES.. 23, 76
TEACHERS:
    Assistants must hold license................................ 53, 75
    Assistants must have contract................................. 53
    Cannot suspend pupils... 63

TEACHERS—*Continued*.

Causes for revocation of license	36, 37
Certificates, grades of	21, 37
Certificates cannot be renewed	38
Certificates, valid, for how long	38
Certificates expiring while teaching, effect of	73, 74
Characteristics of good teachers	34, 35
Examination of	35
License expiring while teaching, effect of	73, 74
May have license revoked	36, 37
Moral character of	36
Must pay fees to county treasurer	32
Must contract with directors	52, 53, 54, 75
Must hold license	52, 73, 75
Must use register	55, 75, 75
Must be reported by directors	61
Must report infraction of rules	63
Must be examined	35, 36
Must believe in a supreme being	36
Must teach common school branches	37
Must be re-examined, when	38
Must attend county institutes	76
Must not permit sectarian teaching	77
Must not be charged for loss of time, when	76
Penalty for failure to report	77
Penalty for teaching without license	73, 74, 75
Power as to rules	65, 66, 67
Power as to corporal punishment	66
Superintendent must hold license when	54, 73, 75
Superintendent must have contract	54, 75
What teachers must report	55
With certain vices, may not teach	36
Wages, how affected by revocation	37
Removal of	37, 87

TEXT BOOKS:

State superintendent to prepare list of	22
Directors to adopt	55, 86

TAXES:

How voted and levied	13, 43, 46, 47
How collected	13, 47, 71, 72, 73

TREASURER:

State	22, 36, 120
County	22, 36, 78, 79, 80

TREASURER—*Continued*.

    Orders of directors upon 59, 74
    Duties as to funds of transferred children 71, 121, 122
    Commission on school fund 102

TRANSFERS:

    General power 25, 70, 121, 122
    Colored children, ten or less 71
    White children, ten or less 71
    Taxes of 72, 121
    Rights of 72

TRESPASS 78

U

UNIVERSITY:

    Power to support by taxation 11

V

VACANCIES:

    In office of Superintendent of Public Instruction 21
    In office of examiner 41
    In office of director 49, 83

VISITATION:

    Of directors 55, 56
    In separate districts 86, 90

VIOLATIONS OF SCHOOL LAW 80

WARRANTS 59, 78, 88

    Statutes of limitation run against 59

www.ingramcontent.com/pod-product-compliance
Lightning Source LLC
Chambersburg PA
CBHW022122160426
43197CB00009B/1118